Dream Life, Wake Life

Dream Life,

THE HUMAN CONDITION

Wake Life

THROUGH DREAMS

Gordon G. Globus

State University of New York Press

SUNY Series in Transpersonal Psychology
Richard D. Mann and Jean B. Mann, Editors

Published by
State University of New York Press, Albany
© 1987 State University of New York
For information, address State University of New York Press, State University Plaza,
Albany, N.Y., 12246

Library of Congress Cataloging-in-Publication Data

Globus, Gordon C., 1934-
   Dream Life, wake life.

   Bibliography: p.
   Includes index.
   1. Dreams.   I. Title.
BF1078.G46 1987   154.6′3   86-30036
ISBN 0-88706-358-6
ISBN 0-88706-359-4 (pbk.)

BF
1078
·G466
1987

10   9   8   7   6   5   4   3   2   1

Contents

Preface

Some of the bizarre worlds we encounter and crazy things we do in dreams are certainly thought-provoking. Even that we have any such intense life at all, lying quietly there in the dark, makes one ponder. People have probably always puzzled and reflected on their dream lives, and the relevance to their waking lives. There is, for example, a profound tradition of Indian stories about dreamers going back to the *Rg Veda* (c. 1000 B.C.) and the *Upaniṣads* (c. 700 B.C.), as O'Flaherty has so beautifully brought out. Along these general lines, the guiding heuristic principle of the present discussion—my strategy for discovering—is that an investigation of dreaming might illuminate waking.

I best confess at the outset that I have a certain predilection for dreaming. Someone who does not so honor their dreams may think this book strange and incomprehensible. Those who are attracted to their dreams may find this work helpful in appreciating the full significance of their dream life, and thereby have an impact on their waking life too. I do not mean here that my central focus is on dream hermeneutics, on what dreams "really mean," even though that topic comes up frequently. I do not primarily use the dream as entry to the personal unconscious, like Freud, or to the universal unconscious, like Jung, although this is of great individual and clinical interest. My main concern is instead with dreaming and the dream as opening a window on the waking human condition.

The thread of my discussion is picked up psychoanalytically in chapter one, at the point of Freud's great *The interpretation of dreams* (1900). The succeeding chapters pick up the dream thread in different ways, including those of phenomenology, cognitive science, transpersonal psychology and existentialism. By the end of the book we shall have considered some of what such seminal and diverse thinkers as Sigmund Freud, C.G. Jung, Medard Boss, Alan Rechtschaffen, David Foulkes, and Wendy Doniger O'Flaherty have said about dreaming.

Attention is centered initially on accounting for generation of the dreaming life-world. Where does the dream world and our life in it come from? The main critical point of chapter one is the inadequacy of Freud's theory that the dreaming life-world is formed by a compositing of memory traces (mnemic copies) of waking experiences. This life-world is not created by a "syntactical" rearranging of mnemic copies, as Freud would have it, but is instead "formatively" created *de novo* by our own mental acts. We dream-think the dream world like Zeus conceives the fully-armed Athena springing forth from his brow.

As the discussion of dreaming moves forward, some implications for the wake life are developed. In chapter two the phenomenological description of dreaming is compared with waking. It turns out that dreaming and waking lives are indistinguishable *as unreflectively lived lives.* Chapter three then attempts to drive home the following rather scary conclusion. Both lives demand the same explanation on grounds of parsimony and evolutionary selection, and so if the dream life is "formatively created," then so is the wake life. We think up the very life-world of waking too. We are enclosed within a "bubble of perception" of our own making, as Castaneda's sorcerer says. Our true condition is monadic.

Formative creativity is explored in a different way in chapter four. Proceeding within the general frame of cognitive science, the main issue becomes the kind of machine that might create *de novo*. In the critical phase of chapter four it is seen that machine "synthesis" of life-worlds guided by analysis of input is an empty notion. "Possible worlds" machines that have a capacity for formative creativity are discussed in the constructive phase of this chapter.

The final two chapters attempt to bring a better balance to the overall discussion. In the earlier focus on scientific approaches to dreaming as found in Freud and Foulkes, the human condition could not be seen in full dimensionality. Chapter five works to correct this by discussing dreaming from a Jungian transpersonal frame. The dream can be oracle, expressing wisdom, rather than raw wish. There is a mysterious dimension to our lives, when we open up to it, that can be clearly seen in relation to dreaming. The final chapter expands the discussion in an existential way. We are for Heidegger that most peculiar being (entity) for whom its own Being (existence) is at issue; however, we seem to haven an awful bootstrap problem in getting the issue settled. Looking over to our sometimes fantastic dream existing provides perspective, an Archimedes' point, from which to launch the bootstrap operation.

Although my synopsis of the six chapters sounds like a nice linear progression, the movement is actually much fuzzier, more of a spiraling than a line. I think this is the proper movement for truly interdisciplinary endeavors, where understanding moves forward through moving back and forth between disciplinary frames. Those who hate machines can safely skip chapter four, those who loathe anything smacking of "mysticism" can easily bypass chapter five, and those who just detest Heidegger can detour around chapter six without losing the thread. Thus my own interdisciplinary and irenic tendency toward accommodating everyone need not be followed by the reader.

The tone of my discussion is sometimes personal, since following Freud's example in *The Interpretation of Dreams* but in a more phenomenological vein, I reflect on my own dreams which relate to the various existential crises that happened during the period of this writing ("in the unbearable lightness of being," as Kundera says). In seeking knowledge of the human condition through dreaming, there is just no substitute for consulting one's own. So my own "dream life, wake life" is integral to this book. I hope that the reader will be motivated to reflect on his or her own dream life and its implications for the wake life coordinate with the reading.

Capistrano by the Sea Hospital
Dana Point, California
Summer, 1986

Citations

In order to not clutter the text, citations are handled as follows. Names occurring in the text without any notation can be assumed to have clear-cut reference in the Bibliography. All other citation details are given in the Notes. Names in the text are sometimes followed by the year of a reference to indicate an historical period or single out a seminal reference relevant to understanding the text.

The author gratefully acknowledges permission to quote excerpts from the following sources: THE INTERPRETATION OF DREAMS, Volumes 4 and 5. The Standard Edition of the complete psychological works of Sigmund Freud, translated and edited by James Strachey. Published by Basic Books, Inc., by arrangement with George Allen & Unwin Ltd. and The Hogarth Press, Ltd.

ON DREAMING. AN ENCOUNTER WITH MEDARD BOSS, edited by C.E. Scott. Published by Scholars Press.

THE PSYCHOANALYTIC STUDY OF THE CHILD, Vol. 27, "Language and Dreams" by Marshall Edelson. Published by Yale University Press.

Acknowledgements

I thank Bill Cooper for suggesting that I think about possible worlds logic, and keeping up a conversation on it. I am grateful to Betty Smith for curing my aversion to Jung, and some suggestions regarding chapter five. Residents in my dream seminar—Melissa Derfler, David Dobos, Stephen Pituck, David Rupley and David Sibley—helped greatly improve the manuscript in its late stages.

I thank Hal Day and Capistrano by the Sea Hospital for support and an interesting environment.

Major portions of the book were written while on sabbatical in Mendocino County. I thank Mendocino friends for their good energy.

The editorial understanding and assistance of Sue Hemington was invaluable. I thank Jeanne Reiss for making my administrative life enjoyable. "Your loves, as mine to you."

For the sixteenth *nagual*

. . . it may be concluded that dreams are not sent by God, nor are they designed for this purpose (to reveal the future). They have a divine aspect, however, for Nature (their cause) is divinely planned, though not in itself divine.

Aristotle, *De Insomniis*

Chapter One

The Creativity
of Dreaming

> *Here we have the most general and the most striking characteristic of the process of dreaming: a thought, and as a rule a thought of something that is wished, is objectified in the dream, is represented as a scene, or, as it seems to us, is experienced.*
> Sigmund Freud, The Interpretation of Dreams *(1900, p. 534)*

1.0 INTRODUCTION

Our most creative moments are while dreaming. Even seemingly unimaginative people may experience rich dream lives. There are infinite worlds possible within our dreaming bubble of perception. Dreaming frees us from the actual world to the set of all possible worlds.

I emphasize that the creativity is *ours*. It might be thought that our dream lives just happen to us, that we are catatonic, enraptured spectators of a dream show put on by somebody else. Thus Hobson and McCarley argue that there is some quasi-random, mechanical, computer-like process going on in which a dream-sleepy mind is obliged to stitch together an incoherent batch of memory traces into a story, "making the best of a bad job," as they say.[1] In what follows I shall argue against this mechanistic view, claiming that we spontaneously create *de novo* our dreaming life-world.

Since creativity is a fundamental characteristic of human beings, an appreciation of its nature is of great importance. If I think that I am creative in the way that this word processor at which I type is creative, then my self-image is gravely distorted; I would limit myself in virtue of my thoughts about myself. So becoming clear about creativity is essential. I think that the study of dream creativity is a very direct route to understanding the true creativity of which human beings are capable.

1.1 BACKGROUND

Twentieth century discussion of dreams has been dominated by Freud's classic monograph, *The Interpretation of Dreams*, which was published in 1900. It is true that Freud's name is no longer something to conjure with, as it was in the fifties and sixties, and even within psychoanalysis there have been great changes in the classical Freudian approach. If anything, it is fashionable among all but the orthodox to curl their lip a bit at poor Vienna-bound Freud. However, the discoveries of Freud's *The Interpretation of Dreams* remain canonical. Freud himself wrote in the preface to the third English edition that "Insight such as this falls to one's lot but once in a life-time." To appreciate the magnitude of Freud's originality, recall that in making dreams his data base, Freud took something that hardly anyone was serious about in *fin de siecle* Europe and America. Furthermore, this data was conveniently available to everyone first-hand each night, and also easily available second-hand from others just for the asking (since most everyone loves to talk about their dreams). Freud's approach was thus strikingly fresh and economical.

There was moreover hardly anything insightful written on dreams before Freud, so the field was quite uncluttered. In his introductory lectures on psychoanalysis, Freud captures the prevailing sentiments towards dreams.

But to concern oneself with dreams is not merely unpractical and uncalled-for, it is positively disgraceful. It brings with it the odium of being unscientific and rouses the suspicion of a personal inclination to mysticism. Imagine a medical man going in for dreams when there are so many more serious things even in neuropathology and psychiatry—tumors as big as apples compressing the organ of mind, haemorrhages, chronic inflammation, in all of which the changes in tissues can be demonstrated under the microscope! No, dreams are much too trivial, and unworthy to be an object of research. (Freud, 1917, p. 84)

So unpromising was the state of the art for dreams that Freud left his literature review (chapter one) to the very last, and belly-ached about doing it. Although he is very generous to previous writers on dreams in his concluding chapter seven, Freud in fact felt quite differently. He wrote to his friend Wilhelm Fliess that he had found only one sensible remark (by Fechner) in the whole literature review on dreams. Thus, there was readily available data, both from Freud's dream life and his patients' dream lives, and the domain was a virtual *terra incognita*. It was Freud's genius to exploit this opportunity for the exploration of the mind through the systematic study of dreams.

Freud's dream theory was central to his constructing an extraordinarily comprehensive theory of the mind that covered not only dreams but clinical ("psychopathological") phenomena and normal waking life as well, embracing all of mind. But here Freud's interest took a decisive turn. His primary fascination was with the unconscious in *The Interpretation of Dreams*. Near the end of his concluding chapter seven he italicizes the statement: *The interpretation of dreams is the royal road to a knowledge of the unconscious activities of the mind.* Freud was much less concerned with the conscious mind.[2]

The historical context of Freud's emphasis on the unconscious mind at the expense of the conscious mind needs to be appreciated here. The contemporary understanding of consciousness is marked by the work of the great phenomenologist Edmund Husserl (1913, 1931), who was a contemporary of Freud. Indeed, both Husserl and Freud attended Brentano's philosophical lectures at the University of Vienna. Freud and Husserl were nearly innocent of each other, however. Husserl and his followers were quite uninterested in anything so ephemeral and irrational as dreams. Husserl saw his phenomenology as the true beginning of Philosophy; he was after the absolutely certain, and in this "apodictic" quest was not concerned with dreams. So there has not been a concerted effort from phenomenological or psychoanalytic sides to re-late dreams and consciousness.

In the over eighty years since publication of *The Interpretation of Dreams*, there have been many rich footnotes but only a handful of truly seminal contributions to the theory of dreams, I think. Jung greatly ex-panded the horizon of dreams, even to include the phylogenetic uncons-cious as a factor in their construction. But already in Freud's dream book one finds this eloquent statement:

> Nor can we leave the subject of regression in dreams without setting down in words a notion by which we have already re-peatedly been struck and which will recur with fresh intensity when we have entered more deeply into the study of the psy-choneuroses: namely that dreaming is on the whole an example of regression to the dreamer's earliest condition, a revival of his childhood, of the instinctual impulses which dominated it and of the methods of expression which were then available to him. Behind this childhood of the individual we are promised a pic-ture of a phylogenetic childhood—a picture of the development of the human race, of which the individual's development is in fact an abbreviated recapitulation influenced by the chance cir-cumstances of life. We can guess how much to the point is Nietz-sche's assertion that in dreams 'some primaeval relic of humanity is at work which we can now scarcely reach any longer by direct path'; and we may expect that the analysis of dreams will lead us to a knowledge of man's archaic heritage, of what is psychically innate in him. Dreams and neuroses seem to have preserved more mental antiquities than we could have imagined possible; so that psycho-analysis may claim a high place among the sci-ences which are concerned with the reconstruction of the earliest and most obscure periods of the beginnings of the human race. (Freud, 1900, p. 548)

It was Jung, however, who deeply appreciated "man's archaic in-heritance" (as Freud said), its pervasive power as organized into the *archetypes*. Jung was at heart committed to the *a priori*, in the tradition of Kant and Plato, whereas Freud was committed to empiricism.

Furthermore, Jung was more the humanist than the scientist and ac-cordingly saw the dream within a larger cultural and spiritual context than Freud. The rich transpersonal flavor of Jung comes forward in the following quotation:

> The dream is a little hidden door in the innermost and most secret recesses of the soul, opening into that cosmic night which was psyche long before there was any ego-consciousness, and which will remain psyche no matter how far our ego-consciousness may extend. For all ego-consciousness is isolated: it separates and discriminates, knows only particulars, and sees only what can be related to the ego. Its essence is limitation, though it reach to the farthest nebulae among the stars. All consciousness separates; but in dreams we put on the likeness of that more universal, truer, more eternal man dwelling in the darkness of primordial night. There he is still the whole, and the whole is in him, indistinguishable from pure nature and bare of all egohood. It is from these all-uniting depths that the dream arises, be it never so childish, grotesque, and immoral. So flowerlike is it in its candor and veracity that it makes us blush for the deceitfulness of our lives. (Jung, 1953, p. 46)

What a splendid statement about dreams!

The next great original contribution to the theory of dreams, on my recounting, was the discovery by Aserinsky and Kleitman (1953, 1955), and Dement and Kleitman (1957), that dreaming occurs during a specialized, periodically recurring, phase of sleep, termed "REM sleep." ("REM" refers to the rapid eye movements that characterize the state of dreaming sleep. As Foulkes[3] discusses, dreaming occurs in other states too, but during REM sleep has its greatest momentum.) This finding initiated an explosion of laboratory research that has redirected attention towards dreaming as a fundamental biological phenomenon that develops in evolution, and accordingly, directed attention away from dreaming consciousness. REM sleep is found, after all, throughout the viviparous mammals (even the primitive opossum), and laboratory data has in fact proved Freud's psychological theorization wrong on a number of fundamental points, as McCarley and Hobson discuss. For example, the dream is clearly not instigated by unconscious wishes and maintained by the wish to go on sleeping, as Freud thought, but there is an autonomous periodic biological mechanism housed in the pontine segment of the brain stem that brings about REM sleep every 100 minutes or so during the night.[4] Under the banner of empirical laboratory investigation, the deprecatory view of dreams in the research literature of Freud's day—a literature that Freud thoroughly criticized—has even been refurbished. Putting aside such attitudes,[5] it is clear that the findings of the contemporary psychophysiological study of sleep should be assimilated in any discussion of dreams.

Over three decades of sleep research have generated an enormous body of biological, psychological and even parapsychological data, but perhaps the most unexpected finding has been the laboratory demonstration of "lucid" dreaming. According to LaBerge, during lucid dreams

> we become and remain fully conscious of the fact that we are dreaming—and therefore that we are asleep. Thus we are, in a sense, simultaneously both "awake" and "asleep." (LaBerge, 1985, p. 6)

The lucid dreamer is thus "conscious" in the sense that

> you know what you are doing while you are doing it, and are able to spell it out explicitly. (LaBerge, 1985, p. 6)

Although lucid dreaming has long been known, at least back to 8th century Tibetan Buddhism according to LaBerge's historical review, and popularly discussed by Garfield, only recently has it been rigorously, experimentally demonstrated and manipulated through psychophysiological research techniques in LaBerge's work. Lucid dreamers are able to signal when they enter the lucid dream state (by moving their eyes in a previously agreed upon way) and can perform previously agreed upon actions, at a time when psychophysiological recording shows unambiguous REM sleep. For example,[6] when asked to engage in dream sexual activity, the lucid dreamer signals with eye movements in succession the start of lucidity in the dream, the onset of sexual activity, the event of orgasm, and the onset of waking. Physiological changes known to characterize waking sexual activity and orgasm can be recorded at the time the lucid dreamer signals them. Lucid dreaming opens up an entirely new dimension to dreaming as traditionally conceived.

Lucid dreaming has also been approached in a non-experimental way in the writings of Carlos Castaneda on sorcery. (LaBerge is rather disparaging of Castaneda's contribution.)[7] For Castaneda, lucid dreaming is fundamental to sorceric praxis. Castaneda affirms the possibility of developing the skill of lucid dreaming so that infinite dream worlds might be created *de novo*. Consciousness for Castaneda is thus infinitely creative, the life-world we ordinarily know being but a small part of "separate realities" (Tarskian "possible worlds"?) that might be known.[8]

To continue my brief history of seminal contributions to the understanding of dreams, there is the linguistic rendition of Freud's dream theory. This story—in effect entitled "Freud Meets Chomsky"—has been presented both from within psychoanalysis by Marshall Edelson and from the vantage of sleep research by David Foulkes.[9] Freud's dream book lends itself to a linguistic interpretation once the outdated biology (the so-called "economic theory") is stripped away. Indeed, Freud can be considered a progenitor of the contemporary computational theory of mind to which Chomsky has made basic contributions. (Freud was greatly influenced by Helmholtz, whose "unconscious inference" still lies at the core of the computational theory of mind.)

Freud himself, in a linguistic vein, had compared the dream to a picture puzzle or "rebus" at the start of his great chapter six on the dream work. Just as we translate the pictures of the rebus into language (say, a picture of a stone mill by a stream, a path through the woods, and a key = Milwaukee) so are the dream pictures translated into the unconscious dream thoughts (on the proper interpretation and according to the proper methods, of course).

The contemporary psycholinguistic view draws an analogy between the way that unconscious dream thoughts generate the infinite life-worlds of dreams and the way that a grammar "generates" the sentences of a language. *The dream is just a thought expressed* (dominantly, but not exclusively) *in a pictorial rather than verbal fashion.*

I think that the establishment of a connection between Freud's dream theory and cognitive science via linguistics is a crucially important development. *The Interpretation of Dreams* is foundational for psychoanalysis and psychodynamic psychiatry on the one hand, and cognitive science is the cutting edge of the science of mind on the other hand, a meeting place for workers in philosophy, brain science, behavioral science, artificial intelligence, linguistics and related areas. So the work of Edelson and Foulkes builds a creative bridge between Freudian thought and cognitive science.

In more recent work Foulkes (1985) backs off from the psycholinguistic approach to dreams in favor of cognitive psychology, and backs off from Freud as well. The dream narrative is no longer a translated message from wishful thoughts to pictures; instead there is a cognitive plan for dealing with more or less randomly activated memories. The dreamer's wish is only "syntactical," viz. that the memories are composited into the dream in a well-formed, grammatically proper way. So now Foulkes would assimilate dreaming to cognitive science more via cognitive psychology than via psycholinguistics *cum* Freud.

Finally, I want to mention the work of Boss and his "Daseinsanalytical" approach to dreams. Boss brings an existential, essentially Heideggerian, orientation to dreams. This is a less natural extension of Freud than the linguistic and cognitive psychological extensions, for Freud was thoroughly immersed in the "natural attitude" of science, and Husserl had already bracketed all that in his phenomenological method. Boss[10] observes that "no new dream theory could ever have seen the light of day had it not been preceded by the concrete decisive observations of Freud, Adler and Jung," but he quickly adds, "Yet the dream theories of these pioneers lead us astray from the outset . . . " For Boss, at one time a person exists as a waking being and at another time as a dreaming being. Dreaming and waking are

> two equally autochthonous—though very different—ways or possibilities of existing on the part of an always unitary human Dasein. (Boss, 1977b, p. 8)

It therefore follows that dream theory "presupposes an adequate insight into the basic constitution of how we exist."[11] It is apparent that the split between where Edelson and Foulkes take Freud (viz. to Chomsky) and where Boss takes Freud (viz. to Heidegger) reiterates in the dreaming domain the larger split between analytic Anglo-American philosophy and existential Continental philosophy.

I draw upon this past work on dreams as follows. The method of this chapter is to follow Freud's strategy of studying the mind through dreams. But whereas Freud was focused on the unconscious mind, I shall focus on the conscious, creative mind, and attempt to see what dreams can teach us about consciousness and creativity. This is to say that Freud used the dream as *via regia* to the unconscious and I endeavor to take the dream as *via regia* to consciousness and its inherent creativity and ultimately to the human condition.

I by and large accept Freud's clinical interpretation of dreams in the present chapter, although I use a much more formal language. My primary concern here is not with what dreams "really mean" but with how they are created and what this implies about the human condition. I think that Freud, Jung, Boss, Fromm, Perls and many others have already said most of what there is to say about what dreams really mean. I follow Edelson and Foulkes in emphasizing the role of cognition in dreaming. However, my approach is existential-phenomenological rather than linguistic in spirit.

1.2 FREUD'S COMPOSITIONAL THEORY OF DREAM FORMATION

1.2a Introduction

Freud saw with great clarity that dreams are at heart thoughts, *wishful thoughts*. However, despite the intimate responsibility we each bear for our own thoughts, neither the dreaming nor the waking consciousness recognizes the dream to be wishful thoughts, since these thoughts are "unconscious" and expressed only symbolically in a predominantly pictorial script. The question then arises: *Just how is the dream life thought up? What is the mechanism for creating the concrete life-world in dreams?*

This question gains even more cogency when we consider the enormous difference between dreaming and waking thought in this regard. In waking it is quite difficult, and for most of us impossible, just to think up an authentic life-world with all its furniture. Our waking imagination is pale compared to dreams. In dreams we actually feel ourselves perceiving and in instrumental relations with world objects. How, then, does the mind perform this remarkable task of creating an authentic dream life?

1.2b The Dream Life is Second Hand

Freud argued that the dream life has a derivative status; the dreaming life-world is constructed from a lawful arranging of "memory traces" of past waking life episodes. (This lawful arranging is more formally "syntactical" operations of the dream work.) The particular waking episodes that are reflected in the dream via their memory traces are especially "indifferent" impressions from the preceding day (called "day residues") but also impressions from the distant past. Freud showed abundantly that through freely associating to each of the dream elements—seeing what comes to mind without judging its value—one is led to these waking life experiences in a compelling fashion, and so it seems quite plausible that the dream life is but a memory, a composite memory, of the wake life. Thus the dream, however creative, is at heart second-hand for Freud.

I shall call Freud's theory the *compositional theory*, since for Freud the dream life is a composite of memory traces of waking life. A memory trace is described as "a trace . . . left in our psychical apparatus of the perceptions which impinge upon it."[12] That this trace is copy-like is shown by Freud's speaking of the "mnemic image,"[13] of "memories couched in visual form and eager for revival"[14] and of "memories possessing great sensory force."[15] Regarding one of his "most vivid and beautiful" dreams, he remarks, "The beauty of the colours in the dream was only a repetition of something seen in my memory."[16] To emphasize how Freud thought of memory traces, I shall call them "mnemic copies" of waking life.

The fantastic quality of the dream is a function of the special ways these mnemic copies are combined. The dream is thus "a mass of . . . composite structures."[17]

> The possibility of creating composite structures stands foremost among the characteristics which so often lend dreams a fantastic appearance, for it introduces into the content of dreams elements which could never have been objects of actual perception. The psychical process of constructing composite images in dreams is evidently the same as when we imagine or portray a centaur or a dragon in waking life. The only difference is that

what determines the production of the imaginary figure in waking life is the impression which the new structure itself is intended to make; whereas the formation of the composite structure in a dream is determined by a factor extraneous to its actual shape—namely the common element in the dream-thoughts. Composite structures in dreams can be formed in a great variety of ways. The most naive of these procedures merely represents the attributes of one thing to the accompaniment of a knowledge that they also belong to something else. A more painstaking technique combines the features of both objects into a new image and in so doing makes clever use of any similarities that the two objects may happen to possess in reality. The new structure may seem entirely absurd or may strike us as an imaginative success, according to the material and to the ingenuity with which it is put together. If the objects which are to be condensed into a single unity are much too incongruous, the dream-work is often content with creating a composite structure with a comparatively distinct nucleus, accompanied by a number of less distinct features. In that case the process of unification into a single image may be said to have failed. The two representations are superimposed and produce something in the nature of a contest between the two visual images (Freud, 1900, p. 324-325, p. 325)

Freud gives numerous examples of such composite structures. Here is a marvelously "Freudian" one.

In a dream recorded by Ferenczi, a composite image occurred which was made up from the figure of a *doctor* and of a *horse* and was also dressed in a *nightshirt*. The element common to these three components was arrived at in the analysis after the woman patient had recognized that the nightshirt was an allusion to her father in a scene from childhood. In all three cases it was a question of an object of her sexual curiosity. When she was a child she had often been taken by her nurse to a military studfarm where she had ample opportunities of gratifying what was at that time her still uninhibited curiosity. (Freud, 1900, p. 325)

Freud also observes about composite structures:

> In composition, where this is extended to persons, the dream-image contains features which are peculiar to one or other of the persons concerned but not common to them; so that the combination of these features leads to the appearance of a new unity, a composite figure. (Freud, 1900, p. 293)

Thus, in Freud's dream of Irma,[18] Irma appeared to have a diptheritic membrane, which properly belonged to Freud's eldest daughter. Dr. M of that same dream bore the name, acted and spoke like Dr. M, but his physical characteristics and malady were those of Freud's brother. The single feature of pale appearance was common to both Dr. M and Freud's brother. Yet another sense of composition for Freud entails a kind of averaging.

> I did not combine the features of one person with those of another and in the process omit from the memory-picture certain features of each of them. What I did was to adopt the procedure by means of which Galton produced family portraits: namely by projecting two images on to a single plate, so that certain features common to both are emphasized, while those which fail to fit in with one another cancel one another out and are indistinct in the picture. In my dream about my uncle the fair beard emerged prominently from a face which belonged to two people and which was consequently blurred . . . (Freud, 1900, p. 293)

The analogy to Galton also shows that Freud thinks of memory traces like photographic copies.

That the dream composition is both creative and second hand in Freudian theory is brought out beautifully by Edelson's linguistic formulation. Memory traces are conceived to be like a stock of material at hand which the dream activity ("dream work"), functioning like a *bricoleur*, fashions into a work of art.

> Freud's emphasis, choice of words, and many examples suggest in fact that he considers the production of the dream as an analogue of the artist's activity or (perhaps more appropriately, since he thought there were significant differences between a dream and an artwork), as one of my students has suggested, of

the activity of the bricoleur described by Levi-Strauss in his discussion of mythical thought as a kind of intellectual bricolage—
the *bricoleur* "who works with his hands and uses devious means
compared to those of a craftsman," who, while "adept at performing a large number of diverse tasks . . . does subordinate
each of them to the availability of raw materials and tools conceived and procured for the purpose of the project," but who
makes do "with 'whatever is at hand,' that is to say with a set of
tools and materials which is always finite and is also heterogeneous because what it contains bears no relation to the current
project, or indeed to any particular project, but is the contingent
result of all the occasions there have been to renew or enrich the
stock or to maintain it with the remains of previous constructions
or destructions," the elements having been "collected or retained
on the principle that 'they may always come in handy'."
(Edelson, 1973, p. 224)

Thus, according to the composition-by-a-dream-work-*bricoleur* theory,
the dream life is second-hand because it is composed of mnemic copies
of the wake life, but this second-hand quality is nonetheless creative
because the mnemic copies are uniquely composed.

1.2c Freud's Semiological Bent

I think that Freud did not give full attention to the manifest life-
world of dreams, and so he was content with his compositional theory,
which seems plausible enough. After all, as a second hand affair the
dream world is relatively uninteresting compared to the primary underlying unconscious dream thoughts that generate the dreaming life-
world. Freud's depreciation of the manifest dream is seen in his calling
the dream elements "ungenuine things," mere "substitutes for something else that is unknown to the dreamer."[19] Indeed,the first rule of
dream interpretation is that "we must not concern ourselves with what
the dream *appears* to tell us . . . "[20] But there are other sources of Freud's
relative disregard. Edelson emphasizes that Freud was at heart a
semiologist, concerned with the underlying symbolic meanings of
dreams, rather than the life-world experienced in dreams. (See also Erdelyi on Freud's cognitive orientation.)

Freud thus established psychoanalysis in the realm of semiotics or semiology, as a science of symbolic functioning, which studies symbolic systems (organizations of symbolic entities), their relations to each other, and their acquisition and use. Psychoanalysis inherently aspires, I believe, to a general theory of symbolic functioning (rather than to a general psychology or a general theory of behavior). (Edelson, 1973, p. 204)

Freud accordingly looked away from the dream life as lived to the abstract underlying unconscious dream thoughts. His task was that of translating from the manifest dream life to these hidden and unavailable thoughts, and so he did not give committed attention to the dream experience as such. Thus, Freud's semiological bent together with his fascination with unconscious thought led him away from the dream life as lived, and the compositional theory meant to account for it.

1.2d The Synthetic Function of the Ego

Now, Freud's theory as stated thus far is grossly deficient without an additional principle (which Freud does not clearly bring forth). The various mnemic copies from which the dream is formed are like pieces of a picture puzzle *but from different puzzles.* Granting for the moment that dream images are composites, they are smoothly integrated composites rather than being all stuck together every which way, like a crazy collage of picture snapshots from one's life photo album. There must be some integrating force—*a synthetic function of the dream work*—that composes the unified life-world perceived while dreaming. If it were not for this synthetic function, there would be no difficulty in discriminating a mishmash dream life from the wake life.

But this places an enormous weight upon the "synthetic function" to somehow take the pieces of different puzzles and make them fit nicely together. The dream work must perform an incredible piece of *editing* for Freud's theory really to work. To my mind, Edelson does not explain this editing in the following quotation.

Principles, which determine the choice of operations used in constructing a symbolic entity, are connoted by such phrases as "pleasure principle" and "reality principle," and such a proposition as "the dream-work is under some kind of necessity to com-bine all the sources which have acted as stimuli for the dream into a single unity in the dream itself." (Edelson, 1973, p. 247)

Such an explanation of how disjointed mnemic copies are formed into a seamless life-world—that there is a "single unity" in virtue of "some kind of necessity"—is just to replace one mystery by a more impenetrable one.

Freud wants a little memory snapshot of A's face and another of B's face, and then the two are Galtonized into an averaged unity. This idea works well enough when the mnemic copies are similar, like faces. But say the composite figure is a doctor and a horse and a nightshirt. How are little memory snapshots to be Galtonized into a doctor-horse ac-tually wearing a nightshirt? We can't average doctors, horses and nightshirts any more than apples and oranges. The Freudian position sweeps all this under the rug of the synthetic function.

Again, consider this dream example.

I am driving a rented car and my colleague "Uncle L." is in the back seat. I see him through the rear view mirror. When the car becomes trapped on a peculiar dirt road leading to a beach we get out of the car and discuss the situation.

Now to my dreaming perception, good old Uncle L. looks and sounds like L., just as he is to my waking perception. But I have never ridden in a car with L. or seen him in a rear view mirror or stood with him on a dirt road by the beach. For Freud's theory, a mnemic copy of L. would have to be composited with mnemic copies of seeing other persons in the rear view mirror and mnemic copies of talking with other persons on dirt roads, etc., etc. How are we to conceive of the process by means of which the copy of L. is seamlessly inserted into the copy of seeing someone in the rear view mirror and into the copy of talking with someone on a dirt road, etc? The compositional theory gives no answer to this question, nor can we think of machines that might accomplish such a feat, or even conceive how it might be accomplished. So even if we grant Freud "memories possessing great sensory force," this doesn't provide much help in fabricating an authentic dream life. All the real work is left to the synthetic function.

1.2e The Causal Theory of Perception Applied to Dreams

The tacit philosophical framework of Freud's compositional theory deserves mention. Freud, who was thoroughly trained in basic and clinical neuroscience, assumed the causal theory perception in his discussion.

> The process of perception was never a topic of central importance to Freud, but it is clear that whenever he touches upon it . . . he adheres to a model which conceptualizes perception in terms of an immediately conscious, veridical mirroring of external reality. (Westerlundh and Smith, 1983, p. 597)

For the traditional causal theory, the waking brain receives input from its external world, processes copies of input in complicated ways, and then there is what Freud called "the mysterious leap" to consciousness. In the case of the dreaming brain, input comes not from the senses (which are of course deadened by sleep) but from memory traces of past perceptions of the world. These mnemic copies are worked on by the brain in complicated ways and finally—insert your favorite solution to the mind-brain problem here—there is perceptual consciousness of the dream world (whatever "perceptual consciousness" and "brain" means to you on your favorite solution).

Freud keeps good company, scientifically speaking, in assuming the causal theory of perception. The brain has been traditionally thought of as an information processing machine that accepts input at its sensory receptor-transducers, processes the input-representations, and outputs consciousness (if consciousness is admitted). The mysterious leap from brain to consciousness is bridged by the empirically well-confirmed *principle of mind/brain covariation.* Whatever "mind" and "brain" turn out to mean and whatever their relationship, however weakly mind "supervenes" on the brain,[21] utopian brain science will affirm that mental events follow neural events. (Crudely demonstrated, change neural functioning by the administration of anesthetic gas and the sentient light goes out.) The covariation of the mental and the neural is thus a contingent fact buttressed by both strong empirical support and deep scientific conviction. Freud, who was deeply committed to the science of his

his time and a neuroscientist in his own right, accordingly accepted the causal theory of perception with its mind/brain covariation.

1.2f Regression of the Mental Apparatus While Dreaming

There is another theoretical complication that the compositional theory entails. The causal theory of perception, extended to include the behavioral actions correlated with that perception, has a certain direction of flow: From input to perception to thought to behavioral action. (This is essentially the Sherringtonian hierarchically organized reflex model.) But Freud's theory has the flow *reversing* in the case of dreaming. Thought does not come from perception and lead to behavioral action but reverts to perception.

Freud's account of the reversal was most ingenious. He said that there was "regression" in the mental apparatus to a more primitive mode of functioning where thought *did* lead to percept. For the infant, thought naturally produces hallucination; the mere perceptual presence of the wished for object is gratifying. Just as the hungry infant hallucinates the wished for breast, according to Freud, the dreamer—regressing to infantile mental functioning while asleep—hallucinates wished-for (albeit disguised) objects. Note that this is a truly prodigious construction on the part of (regressed) thought, to hallucinate an authentic life-world.

1.2g A Contemporary Compositional Theory

It is of interest to compare Freud's compositional theory to a theory proposed by contemporary *critics* of Freud who utilize the findings of biological research on dreams. Hobson and McCarley also emphasize memory traces, but now the dream distortions, which Freud saw as due to a process of compositing memory traces, is a function of a synthetic constructive process by the forebrain. The dream process has its origins in the lower brain regions, brain stem sensori-motor systems "with little or no primary ideational, volitional or emotional content."[22] (So the dream process has basically nothing to do with unconscious thought.) Neurons in the pontine brain stem are supposed to generate information endogenously and automatically by mechanisms that are "largely random and reflex"[23] rather than having psychological meaning. This meaningless brain stem stimulus is processed by the forebrain and matched to meaningful memories.

> Best fits to the relative inchoate and incomplete data provided by the primary stimuli are called up from memory, the access to which is facilitated during dreaming sleep. The brain, in the dreaming sleep state, is thus likened to a computer searching its addresser for key words. (Hobson and McCarley, 1977, p. 1347)

The forebrain is activated periodically, and automatically

> synthesizes the dream by comparing [meaningless] information generated in specific brain stem circuits with [meaningful] information stored in memory. (Hobson and McCarley, 1977, p. 1335, brackets added)

Indeed,

> the forebrain may be making the best of a bad job in producing even partially coherent dream imagery from the relatively noisy signals sent up to it from the brain stem. (Hobson and McCarley, 1977, p. 1347)

So the "largely random" and "relatively inchoate and incomplete" data reflexly generated by the brain stem picks out more or less matching memory traces, and then this jumble of mnemic copies is synthesized into dream images. The difference from Freud is that an active organizing wish is replaced by a quasi-random mechanical process with a superimposed organizing process so that the dream is an essentially meaningless production rather than purposive. Hobson and McCarley thus gut Freud's dream theory and revert to the pre-Freudian theories of dreams, essentially finding them epiphenomena of meaningless, quasi-random, mechanical processes in the brain.

A similar meaninglessly mechanical notion of Crick and Mitchison has the brain stem give the forebrain "a varied pattern of bangs,"[24] which jogs the sleeping brain to activity that cleans up its circuitry of unwanted "parasitic" modes. The dream is thus a by-product of unclogging the memory stores, a kind of reverse learning.

Even though the Hobson-McCarley and Crick-Mitchison theories surely make Freud turn over in his grave, all are in agreement that memory traces provide the raw material for the dream world, and that it is left to unexplained "synthetic" processes to shape that material into a dream. (We will see in chapter four that Foulkes revises this basic line of thought in a highly sophisticated fashion, making use of cognitive psychology.)

1.2h Summary

Freud's compositional theory is thus an internally consistent and respectable theory in which the dream is second hand but has the look of fantastic novelty by virtue of the rules for composing the second hand elements. However, these restrictions and limitations are noted. Freud tacitly assumes the casual theory of perception. He posits a regression of the mental apparatus to an earlier level of functioning such that the normal course of information flow reverses itself. Most crucially, he requires a synthetic function of the dream work with remarkable and unexplained properties.

Furthermore, when we turn to our own dream lives then we find authentically novel elements that cannot be plausibly explained by the compositional theory. In the next section, two dreams are presented to illustrate this critique of Freud's theory. *The reader is invited to co-reflect by examining his or her own dreams,* in order to decide if the dream life is indeed a mere composition of previous waking life episodes. The following illustrations (and those of later chapters) may not entirely convince one that the compositional theory is wrong, but an examination of one's own dream life will, I believe, prove compelling.

1.3 A CRITIQUE OF FREUD'S COMPOSITIONAL THEORY:
TWO ILLUSTRATIONS OF DREAM NOVELTY

1.3a Introduction

I want to consider further the plausibility of Freud's compositional theory through the study of two dreams that contain novel elements.

Can dream novelty be explained by memory trace composition? The issue of plausibility needs to be underlined here, since I think Freud's theory is defensible (to death). The problem is, as we shall see, that his theory becomes quite cumbersome, requiring (1) the ad hoc postulate of unremembered previous life experiences that supposedly serve as sources of the memory traces composited into dreams, and as already noted, (2) the postulate of a mysterious synthetic function that smoothly effects the compositing. If the compositional theory fails, and the dream life is not second hand, then we are left with a primary creativity of the dreaming mind.

The first dream to be considered is a wonderful dream of Freud's and the second is one of my own dreams. (Another dream is considered in similiar fashion in chapter three.)

1.3b Freud's Dream of Riding a Horse

I was riding on a grey horse, timidly and awkwardly to begin with, as though I were only reclining upon it. I met one of my colleagues, P., who was sitting high on a horse, dressed in a tweed suit, and who drew my attention to something (probably to my bad seat). I now began to find myself sitting more and more firmly and comfortably on my highly intelligent horse, and noticed that I was feeling quite at home up there. My saddle was a kind of bolster, which completely filled the space between its neck and crupper. In this way I rode straight in between two vans. After riding some distance up the street, I turned round and tried to dismount, first in front of a small open chapel that stood in the street frontage. Then I actually did dismount in front of another chapel that stood near it. My hotel was in the same street; I might have let the horse go to it on its own, but I preferred to lead it there. It was as though I should have felt a-shamed to arrive at it on horseback. A hotel 'boots' was standing in front of the hotel; he showed me a note of mine that had been found, and laughed at me over it. In the note was written, doubly underlined: 'No food' and then another remark (indistinct) such as 'No work,' together with a vague idea that I was in a strange town in which I was doing no work. (Freud, 1900, p. 229)

Freud tells us that at the time of this dream he had an extremely painful boil at the base of his scrotum, so painful indeed that he was unable to continue working. But he notes:

> There is, however, one activity for which, in view of the nature and situation of my complaint, I should certainly have been less fitted for than any other, and that was—riding. And this was precisely the activity in which the dream landed me: it was the most energetic denial of my illness that could possibly be imagined. I cannot in fact ride, nor have I, apart from this, had dreams of riding. I have only sat on a horse once in my life and that was without a saddle, and I did not enjoy it. But in this dream I was riding as though I had no boil on my perineum—or rather *because I wanted not to have one.* (Freud, 1900, p. 230)

Now Freud, as he characteristically does, turns away from the dream life as experienced to the underlying unconscious dream thoughts that generated it. He "makes an interpretation" of the dream life, which means that pictures are translated into unconscious wishes—and following this translation the pictures are disregarded. Freud is not concerned with the dream life *as experienced* but with the dream life *as unconsciously meant.* For example, in addition to commenting on his wish to be rid of the boil, Freud also comments about how his friend P. had taken over a case—a "highly intelligent" lady— with whom Freud had been unsuccessful. P. had been "riding the high horse" vis-a-vis Freud. Freud identifies the highly intelligent dream horse with the patient. Thus Freud turns away from perceived horse to its unconscious meaning. It should be clear that I by no means am challenging Freud's interpretation of his dream, or Freudian dream interpretation in general. My attention is differently directed—towards the dream world experienced *qua* world and the dreamer's authentic feelings and actions in that world.

Let us focus on Freud's apparently vivid experience of riding a horse. Could that experience be plausibly derived from memory traces of past experiences in which Freud actually rode a horse? Freud tells us that he cannot in fact ride, that he had only sat on a horse once in his life and that was without a saddle, and that he did not enjoy that one horseback-riding experience. It sounds, then, as if Freud's distaste for horseback riding would preclude his having had past waking experiences from which the dream riding could be constructed via mnemic copies. His memory stores of horseback riding are highly impoverished compared to his rich and authentic dream of horseback riding.

It might be said, as Freud did of flying dreams, that perhaps when Freud was a child some uncle had carried Freud on his shoulders while playing "horsey," or Freud had galloped on a broom stick, or ridden a wooden horse on the carousel, or whatever. But mnemic copies of these experiences surely would not be enough to construct the feat of riding reclining and riding straight in between two vans. There would also have to be a whopping synthetic function to construct the actual dream experiences from such memory traces. The "synthetic function" is just a creative homunculus that solves nothing, since now creativity has to be accounted for at the homuncular level.

Perhaps Freud as a child just *imagined* himself riding a horse, perhaps while watching a trick rider in the horizontal position or when someone on the street rode right in between two vans. (The memory trace of just watching someone else ride is of no help; Freud's dream is of riding himself.) Indeed, since what we might imagine and fantasize is virtually unlimited, then the memory traces of these imaginings and fantasies would be virtually unlimited; hence the infinite life-world of dreams. (Freud gives just such an explanation of seemingly lengthy dreams that happen in an instant, as when we have a long dream experience in the few seconds after the alarm goes off; that is, such dreams rely on preconstructed unconscious fantasies.) Dreams, then, might utilize memory traces of past vivid imaginings and fantasizings. But there are serious difficulties with this supposition.

For one, although riding a horse was likely imagined by Freud as a child, there are novel occurrences in dreams that seem unlikely to reflect mnemic copies of childhood imaginings. For example, in the dream to be discussed in 1.31c, there is a movement that I make that is so idiosyncratic I am sure I had never previously imagined it. But more cogently, to posit a previous fantasy or imagining that provides the memory trace for the novel dream occurrence neglects that we easily free-associate from dream contents to well-remembered previous experiences, and it is only these associated experiences that are properly admitted to the dream, out of the methodological primacy of the free-association technique. So it is baldly ad hoc just to posit past unremembered fantasies and imaginings as sources of memory traces, *unless they have been picked out by free association.* Let us look more closely at Freud's free associations to riding the dream horse.

The poultice for his boil was like the horse's saddle, he tells us. The grayness of the horse "corresponded precisely" to the salt and pepper color of the suit his colleague P. was wearing last time they met. P. had been successful with one of Freud's treatment failures, and "liked to ride the high horse" in relation to Freud. Freud had "pulled off some remarkable feats" with this patient, which he connects to the feat of trick-riding tangentially at the start of the dream. And this marvelous free association about the patient:

> But in fact, like the horse in the anecdote of the Sunday horseman, this patient had taken me wherever she felt inclined. (Freud, 1900, p. 231)

Strachey's footnote to this dream association picks this anecdote out of a letter from Freud to his friend Fliess, in which Freud describes

> the famous principle of Itzig, the Sunday horseman: "Itzig, where are you riding to?"—"Don't ask *me*. Ask the horse!" (Freud, 1900, p. 231)

So Freud's free associations tell us the waking sources of his experience of riding the dream horse, including sensations of the poultice, the color of P's suit, P's way of relating to Freud, Freud's past feats, the unruly patient, and an anecdote about Itzig, the Sunday horseman. Freud's theory just is that the experience of riding the dream horse is composited out of memories of all this horse stuff.

But consider. The feat of himself riding tangentially like a trick rider is not part of Freud's store of memory traces. *Other kinds* of feats are stored, notably Freud's feats with the patient, but not riding feats. The source of the dream feat pointed to by the free association is something abstract, the concept of feats, of which psychoanalysis and trick-riding are particular instantiations. Freud, of course, has memory traces of his own psychoanalytic feats, not horse riding feats, and so the experience of himself trick riding has no concrete basis in Freud's memory traces, at least as evidenced by his free associations.

Again, consider the color of the horse, which "corresponded precisely" to the salt and pepper of P.'s suit. Freud emphasizes the specificity of the connection, in his association from salt and pepper to highly spiced food, the eating of which has caused his boils, he has been told. But how could the memory trace of a perceptible property of a suit be literally transformed to a perceptible property of a horse? The supposed memory trace of salt and pepper gray is in the form of a salt and pepper gray suit; transforming such a starting material as a gray suit into a gray horse is as hard as making a silk purse into a sow's ear. The connection between the salt and pepper gray of the horse and the salt and pepper gray of the suit is instead in virtue of something abstract, the *concept* of salt and pepper gray, universal salt and pepper gray. The concept "salt and pepper gray" can be instantiated in infinitely many ways. In the case of Freud's dream, this particular concept was first raised by the suit of the emotionally important P. and later instantiated in the dream horse, as one of its perceptible properties, but the concept does not include raw material for its instantiation. Concepts are empty.

The association to P's "riding the high horse" vis-a-vis Freud and the anecdote of Itzig are of no help in providing raw materials to be formed into the dream experience of riding a horse. Only the universal horse is raised through those associations, but nothing that might serve as basis for the actual experience of riding a horse. Finally, although the sensation of a poultice is something like the sensation of a saddle, and might even feel quite the same to the REM-sleepy ego, wearing a poultice has only a vague resemblance to riding a horse, and it would take an incredible feat on the part of the synthetic function to transform one to the other. The poultice *qua* saddle-feeling might well raise the issue of riding in the abstract, but in itself, it does not provide memory traces that might be transformable into the actual experience of riding a horse.

So when we look to Freud's free associations, we find definite waking sources of his dream experience, but mnemic copies of these sources do not plausibly provide a raw material for the synthetic function to shape into the dream experience. And positing unremembered fantasies from childhood as the source of mnemic copies is a desperate ad hoc move to save the theory. Instead we shall see that the connection between waking sources and dream life is abstract; there are specifications that each life meets in its own way.

1.3c A Dream of Operating Medical Equipment

I am sitting in front of and operating a piece of medical equipment, something like an EEG machine but with a series of padded levers projecting out from the machine. There are 5 or 6 of these levers sticking out from the front of the machine and 2 more sticking out from the left side. I operate the machine by hitting down on the levers from right to left with the underside of my left fist in a particular sequence [which to clarify the following exposition I will code: 1, 2, 1, 2; 3, 4, 5, maybe 6; 7, 8, 7, 8]. The first two levers are close together; I hit them in sequence and then repeat the sequence (1,2,1,2;). Then there are 3 or 4 levers, each of which I hit once, still moving from right to left (3,4,5, maybe 6;). Finally, I somewhat awkwardly reach out around the corner of the machine and hit the last two levers, which are close together, and then repeat hitting these last two (7,8,7,8). I keep repeating the whole sequence—*1,2;1,2 / 3,4,5, maybe 6 / 7,8;7,8*—trying to master the rhythm of operating the machine, but I can never get it quite right. My movements of operating the machine are exceptionally vivid and compelling, especially hitting the pairs of levers at the beginning and the end of the sequence, except for the dubious sixth component.

On awakening from the dream, there was no question but that the peculiar dream movement resembled a movement I had actually made during the dramatic experience of a rude awakening that very night, a resemblance that provided prima facie evidence that the dream is second hand. I had been sleeping on the floor in an unaccustomed place on the first night of a vacation, and feeling a cold coming on when I went to bed, I had thoughtfully placed a box of tissues on a cinder block a few feet away from the makeshift bed. (At home I kept a box of tissues on the night table right next to the bed.) I awakened violently and wetly sneezing some time during the night, and dazedly reached out into the pitchblack with my left hand in order to find the box of tissues in its accustomed place on the night table next to the bed. Instead, the underside of my left hand hit the floor, and I paused in confusion. I then groped around in the dark 3 or 4 times, desperately trying to find the box with my hand but only bumping into the floor—until I finally remembered where I was and that I had placed the box of tissues rather distantly. I awkwardly—while still imperatively sneezing!—lunged way out into the cold darkness until my hand hit the box. The movements of operating the dream machine is surely "something like" the movement of trying to reach the box of tissues to cope with the trauma of my sneezing attack, in line with Freud's compositional theory.

Although my bizarre dream movement was far more like that particular waking movement than any other waking movement I can remember making (or even imagining) in my life, nevertheless these movements were not the same. The dream movement was a hitting that was quick, precise and rhythmic, whereas the waking movement was a reaching that was slow, clumsy, and incoherent. The levers I hit were arranged in a neat line with the last pair around a corner, whereas the locations where I hit the floor were without corners and rather scattered, with the last more distant. Although there was an abstract resemblance—a similarity in organizational structure—between the dreaming and waking movements, groping around in the dark for a box of tissues while flat on one's back and violently sneezing just is not the same as sitting in front of a piece of medical equipment and performing precision "hitting" movements to a methodical rhythm.

Let us focus down on a prominent difference between the dream and the wake movement in order to see if the dream movement was in fact second hand. There was a notable pairing component to the dream movement that was absent from the wake movement. The latter went "1 (the first hit punctuated by confusion); 2,3,4, maybe 5 (the groping about); 6 (the lunge)" whereas various kinds of pairings abound in the sequence "1,2;1,2 / 3,4,5, maybe 6 / 7,8;7,8."

Now it happened that a piece of medical equipment and a pair had figured most prominently—indeed *traumatically*—in my life several days prior to the dream. I had been so busy with preparations for leaving home that I had not had "a good night's sleep" since this traumatic event. The trauma had occurred when I had accompanied my pregnant wife for a sonogram at a local hospital. The apparatus for sonography was a very elaborate piece of medical equipment, something like an EEG machine only more complicated. I had been impressed with how deftly the technician's hands had flown over the apparatus, changing the dial settings, while a remarkable picture developed on the screen. A beating heart slowly came into focus and then something else . . . a second beating heart . . . *twins*!

I was barely reconciled (at what I considered my advanced age) to having one baby, but two was far more than I had bargained for. I felt bewildered and overwhelmed. I called my administrator for some emotional support, but she blithely told me that I was fortunate to have enough money to hire help. I began to feel angry and resentful, but could not voice this to my wife, whom I felt obliged to support even though she seemed to be taking the twins in stride. With all the turmoil of preparing to leave on vacation, I simply suppressed my resentful feelings, and had not even had opportunity to "sleep on them" until the night of my dream.

It seems clear from my associations, then, where the prominent pairing in the dream movement comes from. The traumas of seeing the pair of hearts on the sonography screen and the violent, wet sneezing while unable to find the box of tissues had somehow combined. The wake movement had the twins added to it, in the sense that "two of a kind" stood out in the dream movement. But how could the mnemic copy of the waking movement be *composited* with the mnemic copy of perceiving the paired hearts on the sonography screen so as to produce the dream movement? Such a composition is unintelligible. The waking event of the twins had something fundamentally to do with the dream movement, but not in the way the compositional theory would have it. Something else must be going on other than the compositing activity of a dream work *bricoleur*. It was not the mnemic copy of two hearts but the *abstract concept of a pair* that figures in the dream.

Another prominent feature of this dream is the peculiar piece of medical equipment with the padded levers sticking out from the front. Although something like the sonography machine or an EEG machine in overall shape, I had never seen such a bizarre piece of apparatus before in my life. However, on freely associating, the padded lever reminded me of a padded lever that I had seen once before in waking life. As a boy, I lived near the carnival grounds and often hung around there when a carnival was in town. I can recall a machine for testing "manly strength"

that had a padded lever something like that in the dream. You were supposed to hit down on this lever with your fist as hard as you could
possibly hit it, and then a very prominent display would indicate your
level of strength—from weakling to he-man—for all to see. I had always
been afraid to try the machine, fearful that I would publicly come out
a weakling.

This memory also had a certain association to my more recent waking life. I had been surprised and amused at the response of several of
my colleagues when I announced that we were going to have twins.
They saw it as a very *macho* thing to have accomplished, and there were
coarse jokes about my masculine potency. Although I modestly attributed the twins to purely chance genetic factors, I was secretly quite
pleased at my virile public status.

At first blush, the dream machine would seem to be an excellent example of just what the compositional theory is supposed to explain. The
dream machine appears to be a composition of the sonography apparatus and the carnival device. But the levers were not exactly like the
carnival device and also they were fit perfectly to the medical apparatus,
as if they were integral to it and belonged there. The dream machine was
not as if a picture of the sonography apparatus had stuck onto it eight
pictures of the carnival padded lever (like a rebus might have, in sur-
realistic fashion). It was in my dreaming experience of it, a perfectly bona
fide piece of medical equipment that I was extremely serious about
operating. So the task facing the synthetic function is formidable, if the
REM-sleepy ego is to smoothly composite the memory traces of the
sonography apparatus and the carnival device into a coherent dream object. Again, something abstract seems to be involved—the concept of
medical equipment, the concept of padded levers—rather than mnemic
copies of particular pieces of machinery.

1.3d Summary

Even though the dream life is novel, it is surely in some sense a
function of the wake life; the dream life and the wake life do bear a
resemblance. The compositional theory, which posits a combining of
memory traces of waking life by the dream work's REM-sleepy synthetic
function, provides a strained account of that resemblance, but this goes

unremarked in Freud's theory, which focuses on unconscious meanings. This lacuna in Freud's dream theory but mirrors a deficiency in his larger theory of the mental life: Freud gives scant attention to the life-world in waking. What we see is what we see for Freud. What is of more interest is hallucination, where what we see really isn't there. (Indeed, it was not until 1939 that Heinz Hartmann gave perception the dignity of independent conceptual status as an "autonomous ego function.") Freud was, I believe, a common sense man with regard to the life-world of both waking and dreaming. He simply did not find an intriguing problem there.

But we are faced with something quite miraculous in the case of dreams. A fantastic yet authentic life-world is constituted in an apparently infinitely creative operation—and all in the absence of any input! *How is this done? Just what is the relation between waking episodes and the dream life?* For the Freudian theory, the answer to these questions is quite straightforward: The fantastic life-world in dreams is constituted in the absence of input *now*, but there are copies of past input now available, and the life-world is constituted out of these copies. But if the dream is not second-hand under the auspices of a dream-work *bricoleur*, then the answer to these questions may prove to be deeply illuminating.

1.4 A Critique of Edelson's Version Of Freud's Compositional Theory

1.4a Introduction

The essential criticism of the compositional theory brought forth in 1.3 is as follows. The fundamental psychoanalytic technique of free association points to specific waking experiences that are sources of novel dream worlds. But mnemic copies of these waking experiences, even though they resemble the dream experiences, are not plausibly compositable into the novel dream experience, unless a synthetic function is baldly posited that just accomplishes the feat. The issue of how memory traces of waking experiences are transformed into novel dream experiences is then simply transposed to the issue of how the synthetic function actually works. The task of the synthetic function is eased considerably if there are posited past imaginings and fantasies, whose memory traces can be composited into the dream. But this assumption violates the methodological primacy of free associations in psychoanalysis, and moreover, there are dream experiences so idiosyncratic that their having been previously imagined or fantasized is quite implausible. So although Freud is correct in pointing to the *resemblance* between past waking experiences and the dream experience, his compositional theory does not account for this resemblance. Even in the cases where the dream experienced is not novel, there is no account of how the mnemic copy is seamlessly inserted into the dream world. A mysterious synthetic function is left to do the job.

The present section continues the critique of Freud's theory, but as Freud is translated to Chomskyan terms by Edelson. The same critique already developed applies to Edelson's formulation, but the formal character of the compositional theory is brought forward by Edelson's illuminating presentation.[25] Since discussion becomes somewhat technical, the reader may wish to skip to the summary in 1.4e.

1.4b The Dream As Rebus

We have seen that for Freud unconscious dream thoughts are expressed in visual terms as compositions of mnemic copies. In Edelson's self-described "revisitation" of Freud's *The Interpretation of Dreams*, there is a semantically interpreted deep structure that generates a surface structure pictorial representation which is a composite of mnemic copies. We next consider Edelson's argument in detail.

Edelson points to a very significant analogy Freud draws between the dream and a rebus (picture puzzle) in accounting for the representation of latent thoughts by perceptual experiences. A rebus can be defined as

A mode of expressing words and phrases by pictures of objects *whose names* resemble those words, or the syllables of which they are composed; hence, a form of riddle made up of such representations. (Webster's New Collegiate Dictionary, italics added)

Freud's analogy between the dream and a rebus is as follows:

> The dream-thoughts and the dream-content are presented to us like two versions of the same subject-matter in two different languages. Or, more properly, the dream-content seems like a transcript of the dream-thoughts into another mode of expression, whose characters and syntactic laws it is our business to discover by comparing the original and the translation. The dream-thoughts are immediately comprehensible, as soon as we have learnt them. The dream-content, on the other hand, is expressed as it were in a pictographic script, the characters of which have to be transposed individually into the language of the dream-thoughts. (Freud, 1900, p. 311)

There are two features of this analogy that need emphasis. There is a rule-governed translation from one language into another in the case of dreams, but secondly, in so translating, there is also a fundamental change in the kind of primitive bearer of the language, from words to pictures. (A translation from English to French, say, does not entail such a change in primitive bearer, which is linguistic in each case.)

1.4c Translation in Dreams and Language

Now, there is something very similar to the dream thought-dream picture translation going on in the case of language, Edelson says, where there is a translation from a "deep" to a "surface" structure. More specifically, there is a semantically interpreted abstract "deep structure," that generates (according to the semantic and syntactic components of the grammar) an infinity of surface structures that can be concretely realized (according to the phonological component of the grammar) in speech. That is, there is a transformation of the deep structure to the surface structure and also a change in primitive terms from abstract rules and representations to concrete sounds, which is reminiscent of Freud's analogy that there is a translation from one language to another and also a shift in the means of representation.

We may say, then, that thoughts are represented by dream pictures or pictographs, rather than phonologically as in language. It follows that a major difference between language and dreams is the difference between the phonological component—which assigns a phonological representation to transformations of semantically interpreted deep structures through the operation of a set of rules specifying acceptable combinations among a finite set of discrete, differentiable, semantically meaningless sound elements—and that component in the system generating dreams whereby thoughts (semantically interpreted deep structures) are assigned a representation in dream images. The tranformational processes in language and in the system generating dreams, whereby semantically interpreted deep structures become derived surface structures, must also differ, since the former transformational processes must generate a surface structure susceptible to phonological representation and the latter must generate a surface structure susceptible to representation in dream images. (Edelson, 1973, p. 328)

Thus for Edelson the dream work has two components: transformative and representational. In the transformative component, a deep structure thought is transformed to a surface structure, and in the representational component, the surface structure is realized in terms of the dreaming life-world.

1.4d Difficulties in the Analogy Between Dreams and Language

Since Edelson's argument is founded on an analogy, it is important to keep track of where the analogy falters. (As an analogy becomes more "strained," we give less credence to it.) Let us look at the primitive terms of the concrete, perceptually manifest representations of surface structure. Edelson says that the primitive terms are phonemes in the case of language and memory traces in the case of dreams.

... the material utilized in constructing the dream form is not a finite set of discrete, differentiable, semantically meaningless sound elements as in language, but is instead memory images— of past experiences, especially perhaps childhood experiences; of recent experiences; and frequently of apparently trivial, indifferent, insignificant experiences. (Edelson, 1973, p. 229)

Here Edelson notes a difficulty with his analogy: unlike semantically meaningless phonemes, memory images are highly meaningful.

> In the system generating dreams, the component that realizes the dream in perceptible form is not independent of the semantic component (it is unlike language in this regard); (Edelson, 1973, p. 232)

Memory images are analogous not to meaningless phonemes, but to strings of phonemes (morphemes and words) that are meaningful.

I think this disanalogy cuts deeper than Edelson admits. If the elements to be combined are already meaningful, then the surface meaning is not determined solely by the deep structure. The meaningfulness of the elements also contributes to the meaning expressed. In the case of language, the meaning expressed is a function of the deep structure alone; phonemes contribute nothing semantic. This is surely a fundamental kind of difference between dream expressions and linguistic expressions.

Furthermore, the relations between thought and surface representation is entirely arbitrary in the case of language but not for dreams. A particular memory image fragment is used as a means of representation for the latent dream thought because the meaning of the memory image fragment *resembles* the meaning of the latent dream thought.

> ... the memory-image fragment is used to represent meaning either by virtue of the meaningfulness it already possesses as a part of a symbolic entity (i.e. a memory image) or because of other, apparently fortuitous features—certain formal or sensuous properties—which resemble in some way the idea or ideas it is to represent. (Edelson, 1973, p. 232)

In effect, the memory-image fragment is a kind of *symbol* of the latent dream thought by virtue of its resemblance, in terms of cognitive or sensuous meanings, to the latent dream thought.

This resemblance in dreams between the symbol and that signified is entirely at an abstract level. To see this, let us focus down on Edelson's definitions. An abstraction is "a conception or organization of experience, a class or category, an idea or thought."[26] A symbol is "any entity that represents and evokes an abstraction."[27] The symbol thus signifies an abstraction, a conception. When a symbol evokes an abstraction to which its relation is entirely arbitrary, stipulated by rule or convention, then that symbol is a "sign." This is the case for language, which entails an arbitrary relation between sounds-as-signs and conceptual meanings. The dream images, as we have seen, are not symbol-signs, but what Edelson, following Piaget, calls "motivated symbols." Here a symbol and the conception it evokes are

> related by resemblance, that is, when symbol and conception belong with respect to some criterion, property or properties, to the same class or set, *when the symbol is a prototypical exemplar of the conception.* (Edelson, 1973, p. 273, italics added)

Thus the non-arbitrary relation between the latent dream thoughts *qua* semantically interpreted deep structure and the manifest dream images *qua* perceptible representations of surface structures is that there is a resemblance between the respective concepts. The semantically interpreted deep structure specifies a concept, and through this conception selects memory-image fragments that are similarly conceived, which are, indeed, prototypical exemplifications of the deep structural concepts. This is quite disanalogous to the case of language, where the phonological elements are entirely nonconceptual. The complex of deep structures that generate the dream life do so by specifying a set of conceptions which in the viscissitudes of waking life have been perceptibly exemplified, and these exemplifications provide the raw materials for constructing the dream life under the aegis of the synthetic function. It is through the abstract resemblance between the dream life and the latent dream thoughts that the "allusive" property of dreams can be understood. Each element of the manifest dream is an "allusion" in the sense that as motivated symbol it evokes an abstract deep structure.

So the creation of the dream life according to Edelson's Chomskyan translation of Freud goes something like this. There is an abstract semantically interpreted deep structure (latent dream thoughts) that generates (according to the rules of the dream work) a surface structure representation (the manifest life-world of dreams). This surface representation is constructed from a store of memory traces, which provides elements for the construction of the life-world in dreams. The memory traces chosen for the construction are prototypical exemplars of the abstract meanings represented in the deep structures. These memory traces *qua* elements are variously combined, transformed and (somehow) synthesized in a grammatical fashion to form the authentic life-world in dreams. The dream life is accordingly second hand, a mere rearrangement of something *already* formed, a *syntactical creativity*.

But in addition to the strains in the analogy between dreams and languages already mentioned, there now can be seen a more fundamental problem with Edelson's translation of Freud to Chomsky. Chomsky is not at all concerned with the kind of creativity that characterizes dreams. It superficially appears so, since even in his early critique of Skinnerian behaviorism he emphasized the infinite creativity of language, which might be taken as analogous to the infinite creativity of dreams. But Chomsky generally ignores the act of creation on the part of speakers. Because his grammar is termed "generative" (or "generative-transformational"), it is easy to mistake it for creative, but Chomsky's use of "generative" is an odd one. By "generative," Chomsky means a systematic description or enumeration.

> The grammar of the language determines the properties of each of the sentences of the language. For each sentence, the grammar determines aspects of its phonetic form, its meaning, and perhaps more. The language is the set of sentences that are described by the grammar. To introduce a technical term, we say that the grammar "generates" the sentences it describes and their structural descriptions; the grammar is said to "weakly generate" the sentences of the language and to "strongly generate" the structural descriptions of these sentences. When we speak of the linguist's grammar as a "generative grammar," we mean only that it is sufficiently explicit to determine how sentences of the language are in fact characterized by the grammar. The language generated by the grammar is infinite. (Chomsky, 1980, p. 220)

So Chomsky begins with the set of uttered sentences that comprise the language and wants to specify the grammatical rules (syntactical, semantic and phonological) that underlie the construction of this corpus. He distinguishes very sharply[28] between the generative properties of the grammar and the creative aspect of language use.

It is important to bear in mind the fundamental conceptual distinction between generation of sentences by the grammar, on the one hand, and production and interpretation of sentences by the speaker, making use of the resources of the grammar and much else, on the other. The grammar, in whatever form its principles are represented in the mind and brain, simply characterizes the properties of sentences, much as the principles of arithmetic determine the properties of numbers. We have some understanding of the principles of grammar, but there is no promising approach to the normal creative use of language, or to other rule-governed human acts that are freely undertaken. The study of grammar raises problems that we have some hope of solving; the creative use of language is a mystery that eludes our intellectual grasp. (Chomsky, 1980, p. 222)

With this statement Chomsky turns his back on creativity. Now surely dream creativity is analogous to the creativity of speakers, not the "generativity" of Chomskyan grammars, which can describe everything that might be said, including an infinite number of novel sentences, but is not designed to say anything new on its own. An account of something like dream creativity is simply not Chomsky's goal—that account is "a mystery that eludes our intellectual grasp"—and so Edelson's avowed translation of Freudian into Chomskyan terms is fundamentally misguided.

1.4e Summary

Seizing Freud's analogy between the dream and a rebus—in both a pictorial script is to be *retranslated* into thoughts—Edelson attempts a Chomskyan rendition of Freud's dream theory. Dream thoughts generate images analogous to the way that the deep structure of language generates speech. I have argued that Edelson's analogy falters because (1) the elements composited are meaningless phonemes in the case of language and meaningful memory traces in the case of dreams (as Edelson points out), (2) the relation between deep structure and the speech sounds is arbitrary in the case of language, whereas the relation between dream thoughts and the mnemic images that express them is that the latter are prototypical exemplars of the underlying dream thoughts (as Edelson points out), and most crucially, (3) the goals of Chomskyan linguistics are purely descriptive of all the utterances that have been or might be said, whereas Freud's compositional theory is concerned with what is actually produced. Chomsky is concerned with "competence" and Freud with "performance," and in the case of language, performance is according to Chomsky "a mystery that eludes our intellectual grasp."[29] With this difference between Chomsky and Freud, Edelson's analogy collapses.

Even though Edelson's Chomskyan rendition of Freud fails, the formal structure of Freud's theory is clearly brought forth. The specification of just which mnemic copies are to be composited is abstractly accomplished; that is, the mnemic copies chosen exemplify the dream thoughts. Fashioned into the dream, they "allude" to the underlying "dream thoughts." In the work of *forming* a dream, then, the dream thoughts specify mnemic copies to the compositing process, whereas in the work of *interpreting* a dream, the composited memories allude back to the dream thoughts. Thus Freudian hermeneutics intends to return to the cognitive core of dream creation.

In any case, the role of mnemic copies in the formation of dreams is functionally the same in Edelson's Chomskyan version of Freud as in Freud himself. Mnemic copies are (meaningful) raw materials to be composited into the perceptible dream world, akin to the way that (meaningless) phonemes are arranged into perceptible utterances. So the critique of Freud presented in 1.3 applies also to Edelson's Chomskyan version of Freud.

1.5 The Abstract Relation Between the Dream Life and the Wake Life

1.5a Introduction

For the compositional theory, the unconscious dream meanings pick out mnemic copies of perceptible worlds that come under those meanings, that satisfy the unconscious dream thoughts. The copies picked out are then composited into the dream world. Thus the bridge from wake world to dream world is via concrete copies—just those copies that satisfy the dream thoughts. But rejection of Freud's compositional theory has a radical outcome for the theory of dreams. We shall see that the causal connection between wake life and dream life must change from something concrete to something abstract.

1.5b The Equipment Dream and its Relation to the Wake Life

It is remarkable, when naively considered, that in my dream of operating the medical equipment I vividly perceived making a highly complicated movement of my left arm a number of times, even though my sleeping body was immobile. Where did this perception come from? How did it come about that I sensed making such a specific complex movement, if not from a composition of memory traces? Let us consider the "possible worlds" of movement.

Of all the movements I might have possibly made in my dream life that night, a particular movement of the left arm was made, a movement that I attentively experienced myself making (rather than a movement that I made while my mind was elsewhere). Of course, earlier in the night a movement similarly organized had occurred, when I had reached out for the box of tissues with my left arm and couldn't find it. The abstract specification "movement of the left arm" characterizes both the wake life and the dream life. (Note that there are indefinitely many concrete movements that might satisfy that abstract specification.) So this bridge between waking and dreaming is abstract.

Of all the possible submovements of that complex movement of the left arm that I might have made in my dream life that night, a repetitive hitting down with the fist half-pronated was done. The submovement that night was organized into a repeated hitting down with the fist half-pronated. Again, a similar submovement that satisfies this very specification had been made earlier in the night, when my fist hit the floor in groping around for the box of tissues, Also, in the distant past this very specification had characterized an imagined but never effected movement at the carnival. So an abstract specification for submovement—"hit the fist down"—is the same in the waking events picked out by the rule of association and in the dream life.

Of all the possible ways I might have hit down with my left fist half-pronated, I did so with precise control. An operator on the submovement was move "carefully." This specification of movement does not characterize my *movement* organization in the waking life worlds to which I associated (i.e. waking up sneezing, the carnival or the hospital). What "precise control" did characterize was my overall defensive response to the experienced trauma of the twins. I was upset, and hassled trying to get away on vacation, and tired . . . and was desperately trying to control my angry resentment about the unanticipated and unplanned event of having twins. There was a general defensive specification that characterized my waking life: *Be careful to keep everything under precise control.* This abstract specification of waking life shows up again in the organization of the dream movement, which was precisely controlled. The connection is via an abstract entity, viz. precise control (of whatever).

Of all the ways the submovements might have been temporally ordered, the rhythm was divided into three distinct groupings. This rule of temporal organization had been operative earlier in the night when I had reached out expecting to hit the box, then had groped around three or four times trying to find it after my hand hit the floor, and finally had lurched out into the darkness. It is noteworthy here that my waking intention was not to make a rhythmic movement with three major groupings. Each individual submovement was intended to be a terminal movement. It just turned out, as I lived it, that there were 5 or 6 submovements grouped into three phases. What actually happened during waking was conceptualized in three phases—my acts of reaching down, groping around and lurching out—and then the dream movement met the same three-phase specification. Waking and dreaming are linked by the abstract specification: three phases of movement (whatever the movement).

Of all the ways the submovement could be further organized in the first and third groupings, these groupings were perfectly paired in that each comprised a pair of submovements paired. Another specification for movements of the left arm while dreaming that night was thus an imperative: *pair!* My waking life too had come in pairs, when I emotionally and defenselessly perceived two beating hearts come into focus on the sonograph screen. Again, an abstract specification of the trauma in my waking life covers my dream life, which "comes paired." The abstract "idea" of pairs was apparently "on my mind" both waking and sleeping, linking them.

Of all the ways the submovements of the middle grouping could have been organized, there were three or four. Now, the waking middle movement earlier that night had obviously not had three or four submovements. It had three or else it had four. I did not stop to consider how many it had at the time; I just dimly registered three or four groping attempts to find the tissue right by my bed. My perception was blurred, but I didn't care and left it at that. I was just happy finally to find the box of tissues, blow my nose, and miserably roll over and fall asleep. The recurrence of this fuzzy concept in the dream life emphasizes that it was not the submovements that I blurrily wanted to make or actually did make in waking life that provided the specification but how those submovements once made were fuzzily classified by me. The fuzzy specification "three or four movements" provides a bridge between waking and dreaming.

1.5c Summary

There is an abstract connection between the dream life and certain episodes of the wake life. The same specifications bridge the two lives. Not mnemic copies but "mnemic specs" link waking to dreaming.

1.6 THE ABSTRACT RELATION BETWEEN THE UNCONSCIOUS AND THE DREAM LIFE

1.6a Introduction

It was Freud's great discovery that the dream life lives out the fulfillment of disguised unconscious wishes. The dream life is not peculiar in its dependence on the unconscious, since waking life also is riddled with the fulfillment of disguised unconscious wishes. It is just that the true situation of our living out our unconscious wishes becomes especially clear in the case of dreaming. The question then arises: What is the causal connection between unconscious wish and dream life? As in the connection between waking and dream, it is abstract.

1.6b Unconscious Wish, Conception and Plan

Freud understood what I call "the wishful living out of our lives" in a highly cognitive way, as Edelson pointed out. We *think* our lives. Indeed, dreaming is but a special form of thinking—a wishful thinking—

that occurs under the unique conditions of sleep, when the affordances of the external world are nil. Dreaming thought thereby provides a special window on waking thought and life in general, since unconscious wishes are far easier to read in dreams. Accordingly, the true nature of wishful thought can be more easily discerned through the study of dreams.

Now, a wish for Freud is directed towards something that will satisfy the wish, i.e. its "object." The aim of the wish is gratification, which is conceived of as the restoration of that state of affairs which brings pleasure through attainment of the object. We might say, more generally, that the wish is *to feel a certain way* (e.g. feel loved, feel powerful, feel secure, feel sensual pleasure, etc.), and that we each develop plans for obtaining objects and bringing about states of affairs that help us feel those ways. The most important of these plans, at least for the psychopathologist, are unconscious. The person is not conscious that these plans in fact significantly control the living of his or her life (including the "inner mental life"). The person acts within a horizon of meanings that is not known.

Wish gratification requires that something be done, that some plan of action be taken actually to obtain the wished-for object (even if only the hallucination of the object, whose mere perceptual presence is at least temporarily gratifying). To engage in a certain kind of action is to follow certain specifications, wittingly or unwittingly, and over time plans. Thus wishes imply specifications of certain objects and states of affairs, and plans for satisfying those specifications.

The same can be said for defenses against unconscious wishes. Defenses are also plans for living one's life, designed to avoid feeling anxious, guilty, or depressed, which would happen if we acted on our unconscious wishes. Whether defenses provoke counteractions which hold a wishful act in check or provide comforting meanings with which to gloss a situation after the act, defenses imply abstract specifications and plans. Let us consider the dream of medical equipment in regard to unconscious wishes.

1.6c Unconscious Wishes in the Medical Equipment Dream

Given that I am "hitting," it seems likely that unconscious anger is being expressed. But notice, when my hand "hit" the floor while searching for the box of tissues, this was a passive event, not *the act of hitting* that was so prominent in my dream. The *act of hitting* was an expression of "unconscious" angry wishes that were operative in the dream. (These wishes were "unconscious" in the sense that although I knew that I was resentful about twins and could acknowledge it to others, I did not know the extent of that anger, or even more importantly, how it pervaded the living of my life.) When angry, I characteristically want to hit—and in the dream I do hit repeatedly. The passive "hit" of the day residue is transformed to an active hitting in the dream according to the specifications of an unconscious wish that was integral to my waking life.

There are also so-called "phallic" wishes to be admired, powerful and virile, wishes that were also operative in my carnival days, which specified actions I was too bashful, too fearful of ridicule, too insecure, to take. Buoyed by the social approbation of my colleagues over fathering twins, I am finally ready to meet those specifications by operating a machine that symbolizes (alludes to) masculine power. So it is the unconscious aggressive and phallic wishes stimulated by waking experiences (discovering the twins, the approval of my colleagues) that specify transformation of the passive waking hitting to the active dreaming hitting.

Characteristic waking defensive plans also appear in the dream life. In the traumatic experience of watching the two beating hearts come into focus on the sonogram screen, I was passive, defenseless, helpless, without recourse of action, while overwhelmed by stimulation. (I should say, more accurately, that I was overwhelmed by the *meaning* I gave to that stimulation, which was after all only a pair of hearts beating away. My wife gave the pair of hearts a different meaning, and was quite calm about the whole thing!) The plan that I typically follow in defending myself against the anxiety of helplessness and powerlessness is to take assertive action and gain control. After leaving the hospital, I immersed myself in the activities of getting ready to leave on vacation, never dealing with the passive trauma.

In accordance with this plan of actively controlling, my dream life no longer has me the passive witness of an unfolding drama in the sonograph room, a drama in which the fates assigned me the role "father of twins." Now I am the one operating the machine. I am in charge. Again, in my dream life I am not helplessly wracked by copious wet sneezes while I frantically blunder after the box of tissues, but I assert myself in a precise manner. Thus, the passively experienced traumas of my waking life are not reiterated in my dream life but are replaced by an attempt at active mastery through the operation of a plan that prescribes: *take charge*. This plan counters my deep anxiety over passivity. But the trauma is such that the defense does not succeed in controlling either my anxiety or my anger; I cannot get the operation of the dream machine quite right. I keep feeling unsettled. I keep repeating the sequence, in an attempt to master it and thereby relieve my anxiety and anger about not being in control. Moreover, every movement must be *precisely* controlled, according to plan, so that I will not hit angrily and not feel anxious. The "counteraction" against my wish to hit out is that I hit methodically and the "comfortable meaning" of my hitting is that I am not really hitting but operating a piece of medical equipment.

Note there was nothing in the associated day residue or past experience that provided memory traces of actual actions that might be converted to my dream experience of operating the machine. I had only *watched* the technician operate the sonographic apparatus. I have operated pieces of medical equipment in the past—and even hit them a time or two in frustration!—but the actual operation never entailed hitting. And the only machine I can think of that is at all operated through hitting is the carnival machine, and there I had only *thought* of hitting it. So my attempt to master the operation of the machine, and the precise control entailed, derived not from concrete memory traces, but from unconscious wishes and defensive operations whose abstract specifications were integral to my waking life, and continued on into my dream life, where I tried (not quite successfully) to regain perfect, precise, unangry control.

1.6d Summary

Let us briefly survey what has been said so far. Freud's compositional theory makes the dream a second hand composition from waking experience synthesized by a dream work *bricoleur* out of preexisting mnemic copies of particular waking experiences. This theory has been rejected in favor of one in which the connection between the waking and the dream lives is entirely abstract. Abstract specifications, rather than concrete memory traces, somehow mediate between the wake life and the dream life, and abstract rules also mediate between the unconscious and the dream life. We next focus on the resemblance between waking and dreaming lives, and in so doing return to the critique of Freud's compositional theory.

1.7 THE FAMILY RESEMBLANCE BETWEEN WAKING AND DREAMING WORLDS

1.7a Introduction

We saw that for Freud the similarity between the dream world and certain situations in the wake world is because selected memory trace copies of the wake world are composited into the dream world, or the copies are superimposed and averaged over ("Galtonized"[30]). Thus the dream world is rather literally a copy of past worlds, where the memory traces are taken as raw material and composited into the dream world. But when the dream world is novel, as frequently happens, the similarity to the wake world is not literal. There is instead a "family resemblance" between certain past waking worlds and the novel dream world. This section unpacks the concept of "family resemblance" and its relevance to the critique of Freud's compositional theory.

1.7b Family Resemblance According to Wittgenstein

The concept of family resemblance is developed by Wittgenstein (1958) in his *Philosophical Investigations*, where he discusses a kind of resemblance between objects in which the objects recognized as somehow belonging together do not share a core set of traits or features which are "essential" to their resemblance. Wittgenstein is arguing here *against* there being anything in common, some mysterious *essence* (so beloved by Husserl) shared by these objects. There is instead

a complicated network of similarities overlapping and criss-crossing: sometimes overall similarities, sometimes similarities of detail. I can think of no better expression to characterize these similarities than "family resemblance"; for the various resemblances between members of a family: build, features, color of eyes, gait, temperament, etc., etc., overlap and criss-cross in the same way. (Wittgenstein, 1958, sections 66 and 67)

Wittgenstein considers by way of illustration the heterogeneous family of games.

> Consider for example the proceedings that we call "games". I mean board-games, card-games, ball-games, Olympic games, and so on. What is common to them all?—Don't say: "There *must* be something common, or they would not be called 'games' "— but *look and see* whether there is anything common to all.—For if you look at them you will not see something that is common to *all*, but similarities, relationships, and a whole series of them at that. To repeat: don't think, but look!—Look for example at board-games, with their multifarious relationships. Now pass to card-games; here you find many correspondences with the first group, but many common features drop out, and others appear. When we pass next to ball-games, much that is common is re-tained, but much is lost.—Are they all 'amusing'? Compare chess with noughts and crosses. Or is there always winning and losing, or competition between players? Think of patience. In ball games there is winning and losing; but when a child throws his ball at the wall and catches it again, this feature has disappeared. Look at the parts played by skill and luck; and at the difference be-tween skill in chess and skill in tennis. Think now of games like ring-a-ring-a-roses; here is the element of amusement, but how many other characteristic features have disappeared! And we can go through the many, many other groups of games in the same way; can see how similarities crop up and disappear. (Wittgen-stein, 1958, section 66)

There is, then, no essence of games, no absolute basic core of traits across all games, according to Wittgenstein.

1.7c   Dreyfus' Discussion of Family Resemblance

Dreyfus[31] has provided an illuminating discussion of Wittgenstein's concept of family resemblance. We may take the human family as the ex-emplar or paradigm of particular instances that somehow belong together, that are "related" in a kinship sense. Dreyfus observes,

> Family resemblance differs from class membership in several im-
> portant ways: classes can be defined in terms of traits even if
> they have no members, whereas family resemblances are recog-
> nized only in terms of real or imaginary examples. Moreover,
> whereas class membership is all or nothing, family resemblance
> allows a spectrum ranging from the typical to the atypical. An
> atypical member of a family, for example, may be recognized by
> being placed in a series of faces leading from a typical member
> to the atypical one. ... this sort of recognition of a member of a
> "family" is accomplished not by a list of traits, but by seeing the
> case in question in terms of its proximity to a paradigm (i.e. typi-
> cal) case ... (Dreyfus, 1979, p. 126)

It may even be, Dreyfus says, that there are no common traits, not even
overlapping ones.

> Those capable of recognizing a member of a "family" need not
> be able to list *any* exactly similar traits common to even two
> members, nor is there any reason to suppose such traits ex-
> ist ... No matter what disjunctive list of traits is constructed, one
> can always invent a new "family" member whose traits are simi-
> lar to those of the given members without being *exactly* similar to
> any of the traits of any of them ... (Dreyfus, 1979, p. 127)

Although WIttgenstein's own position is somewhat obscure, Dreyfus
makes plain that even the traits or features of a human family disappear
under careful scrutiny.

> A more consistent way of understanding his [Wittgenstein's] an-
> alysis would be to conclude that each of the traits he mentions in
> discussing family resemblance—the build, color of eyes, gait,
> etc.—is not identical in any two members of the family, but in
> turn consists of a network of crisscrossing similarities. (Dreyfus,
> 1979, p. 127, brackets added)

(Of course, when a particular trait is genetically strongly dominant, as may be the case with eye color, then the trait may be identical across family members.)

On Dreyfus' illuminating reading of Wittgenstein, then, the concept of family resemblance becomes phenomenological and there is a return to essentialism.

> Similarity is the ultimate notion in Wittgenstein's analysis and it cannot be reduced ... to a list or disjunction of identical, determinate features. (Dreyfus, 1979, p. 127)

Since similarity is irreducible to a list of particular well-defined traits or features, then we are left with a general likeness or resemblance between family members, the "essence" of the family. Here "essence" no longer implies common features but invariant relationships. I shall depart from Dreyfus in one regard by considering families to be a special type of class, *viz.* the family class. This is just a terminological difference that makes discussion flow more easily without inventing new terminology to replace such terms as "classification" (which is to be understood as "family classification").

1.7d Recognition of Family Members

How, then, do we recognize the resemblance between family members, if this is not done by a list of traits, features or whatever the distinctive property? The answer to this question is that we just do recognize family members as belonging together. There is a "look" we immediately "see" that allows us to classify certain individuals as belonging to the same family. That "look" is primitive and cannot be further analyzed. Our capacity to detect the "look" of the family is remarkably developed, but so commonplace that we scarcely notice it. We look at the newborn and just see the resemblance to this or that side of the family, a resemblance that is maintained throughout subsequent ontogenesis. We immediately classify entirely novel occurrences in a certain family (or families).

This extraordinary capacity appears early in childhood. A 25-month-old twin, who has recognized and distinguished flowers and butterflies for many months, pulls off a pansy petal (which has a shape and color pattern somewhat similar to a butterfly) and then "flies" it around the room while saying "butterfwy." A month later her twin comes upon an "arty" photograph that displays empty clothes lines with a few scattered clothes pins, and exclaims "butterfwy!" The configuration indeed has a highly abstract resemblance to a butterfly, but one that I would have *never* seen unless my attention was called to it.(Nor was it intended by the photographer.) For another example, observing wild ducks paddling down the river, the 25-month-old twins call out "kick! kick! kick!" Their previous experience with "kick! kick! kick!" is that their mother frequently injuncted them in this manner while learning to swim at age one. Subsequently, this became a favorite game, so they would roll over in the bathtub and kick while exclaiming "kick! kick! kick!" and even kick in this manner on the floor. They had also learned to "kick the ball" and had been sometimes admonished, "Don't kick your sister!" Given this repertoire of experiences, it seems quite unlikely that there was some feature or set of features of the ducks paddling down the river in common with the twins' previous experience of "kick! kick! kick!" It seems more plausible to say simply that the ducks "looked" like they were kicking and the twins immediately "saw" the resemblance and made the proper family classification under "kick! kick! kick!" The twins knew the abstract invariant relationships of kicking, not a list of features. The ducks' paddling matched the kicking invariant, and they re-cognized the paddling as kicking.

Dreyfus' point that family members can be ordered as to degree of membership in the family, with certain individual members being *exemplars,* is an important one. If instead of considering how much the kids resemble the dad, we collect pictures of the children and the dad all taken at age 13 *for both children and the dad,* and we make these collections over many family generations at age 13, then we will find exemplary cases of that family line (like the most nearly Hound Dog of the hound dogs in the neighborhood, the near exemplar of Hound *eidos*). Again, the "look" of exemplars is primitive, and cannot be analyzed into a list of features. Certain Smiths just look "very Smith." So we have primitive abilities to family classify and to order family members in terms of the ideal prototype.

1.7e Family Resemblance and the Compositional Theory

Suppose we have two things that bear a "strict" family resemblance, i.e. have *no common elements*. Then there is no way of arranging the elements of one into the other. Syntactical transformation of one thing into another does not work in cases of strict family resemblance. Even when the thing bears a strict family resemblance to many things, selected elements from the many cannot be composited into the thing.

To illustrate, lying in a bed wearing a poultice has a family resemblance to reclining in the saddle of a moving horse. But common postural elements are minimal, if any. Therefore there is no way of syntactically transforming a copy of the one into the other. Again, reaching for the box of tissues while waking has a family resemblance to operating the dream machine. Common movement components of these acts, however, are minimal, if any. So there is no way a purely syntactical operation can transform a copy of the waking movement to the dreaming movement.

Given the typical family resemblance between dreaming and waking worlds, then, Freud's composition theory does not work. This deficiency can be obscured, however, with hand-waving about a miraculous synthetic function that is able to seamlessly fit mnemic images into novel situations (so in my dream I can see Uncle L. in the rear view mirror), able to blend a mishmash of disparate memory traces into an authentic figure (so a doctor-horse comes to wear a nightshirt), and able to shape-to-fit elements of memory traces *before* syntactical operations are performed (so that there can be a family resemblance between lying in bed with a poultice and reclining on a moving horse).

1.7f Summary

The life-world of dreams can bear a "strict" family resemblance to life-worlds of waking. In such cases there are no common concrete elements, and so purely syntactical transformations of waking life worlds cannot yield a dreaming life-world with a strict family resemblance to waking. Accordingly, Freud's compositional theory, which relies on syntactical arrangings of concrete memory traces, cannot account for the life-world of dreams.

1.8 THE FORMATION OF THE DREAM WORLD

1.8a Introduction

My critique of Freud's compositional theory of dream world formation is completed for now. The next task is constructive. So far we have seen only that the link between waking life (including its unconscious wishes) and the dream life is via abstract specifications. What is required next is an account of the causal sequence of events involved in forming the dreaming life world, an account which makes no use of mnemic copies. In order to accomplish this, something first must be said of the biology of dreaming (1.8b) and then the theory of intentionality (1.8c).

1.8b The Biology of Dreaming

There are two easily distinguishable phases of biological sleep, with sharp occurrences of phasic events such as rapid eye movements, designated 'REM' sleep, and without phasic events, designated 'NREM' sleep. Although the dreaming state does not sort out so neatly with the REM-NREM distinction as was first thought,[32] it appears that lengthy, elaborate, vivid, fantastic dreams are the primary province of REM sleep. When a richly elaborated authentic world *is* perceived during sleep (which is by no means always the case), the mechanism of world creation is typically "kicked in" during REM sleep.

Just as the dream life is much closer to the wake life than either life is to non-dreaming sleep, the brain waves recorded electrographically during REM sleep are much closer to the waking EEG than to the EEG of non-dreaming sleep. Both experientially and electrophsysiologically, dreaming is something like being awake. During REM sleep, an authentic dream-life is created by unknown mechanisms (which appear similar to waking mechanisms as grossly evidenced by the EEG).

There is a very dramatic oscillation between the two main phases of sleep, REM and NREM sleep, with often quite sharp transitions between them. Especially in going from NREM to REM sleep, the electrophysiological evidence is very clear that something "kicks in." These transitions punctuate a larger periodicity. In an idealized but nevertheless quite typical sleep sequence, the sleeper falls quickly into a profound NREM sleep (stage 4) and then comes up more slowly to lighter levels of NREM sleep (stage 2), until after near two hours REM sleep kicks in. Sometimes REM sleep does not quite make it; the sleeper "comes up" to stage 2, and then "drops back" to stage 4 without REM sleep ever occurring. As sleep progresses, the deeper NREM stages drop out. In the hours before awakening, REM sleep periodically alternates with stage 2 and bursts of shallow stage 1 NREM sleep. So during sleep, there are periodic recurrences of REM sleep and at those times a (clear or hazy) dream life is constituted.

It should not be thought, however, that the biological function of REM sleep is to produce a dream life. Surely our dream hallucinations do not contribute to survival and reproduction. Perhaps something more primitive and adaptively efficacious is going on, with respect to which dream world formation is a byproduct. Kleitman has proposed that the cycling between REM and NREM phases of sleep reflects a fundamental "basic rest-activity cycle" that is continuous throughout life, waking and sleeping. This basic rest-activity cycle should not be confused with the 24 hour cycle in which rest (sleep) and activity (waking) alternate. The basic rest-activity cycle is a much faster cycle, an "ultradian" rhythm that rides on top of the slower 24 hour "circadian" rhythm. Kleitman adduces considerable evidence that ultradian rhythms in rest and activity are a basic building block that can be discerned in the infant and other animal forms. Ultradian rhythms are markedly damped during adult waking, so it requires special techniques to demonstrate them.[33] But in sleep, the basic rest-activity ultradian rhythm emerges in full force as the REM-NREM intrasleep cycle. What has been selected for in evolution, then, is a fundamental cycle in which *activity is periodically brought about*. There is an over-ride on the cycle during waking, so that activity can be continuously maintained, but in sleep the basic cycle reaches full expression. I suggest that this periodic activation occurs at all levels of functioning, so that even the highest activities of which we are capable periodically "kick in" during sleep. Conceptual activity thus joins rapid eye movements, pontine spikes, penile erection, hormonal spurts and suppressions, and other biological phasic events in the periodic activation of REM sleep.

1.8c The Theory of Intentionality

We have seen that abstract specifications bridge waking and dreaming lives. Both lives fulfill common specifications. But it is we dispassionate observers of a person who see that the person's waking and dreaming come under the same abstract entity. *We* make the link between worlds via something abstract. So the bridge thus far is extrinsic. To give an account of the causal events in dream world formation the "something abstract" must be located within the person's mind. What is required is an account of dreaming in terms of "intentionality".

Now, intentionality is an enormous and convoluted topic in its own right, and one of the central preoccupations of contemporary philosophy. I shall follow Husserl's theory of intentionality here, more specifically, Smith and McIntyre's consistent Fregean interpretation and elaboration of Husserl's theory, which brings Husserl into the contemporary mainstream. I can convey only the barest bones of their discussion.

The distinction between the intentional act and the object upon which the act is directed is fundamental. (This distinction was clearly brought forth by Brentano; however Husserl develops it differently.) But act and object are essentially linked: *All consciousness is consciousness-of-_____*. In the case of perceiving, the act is mental, "immanent" to mind, a consciousness-of, whereas the object is physical, "transcendent," the substantial object of consciousness. The intentional relation between act and object thus crosses an ontological gap between immanent and transcendent (which brings all kinds of difficulty to theories of intentionality).

This perceptual act is guided by *meanings*. The meanings (*noematic Sinne*) "prescribe" the world object towards which the perceptual act is directed. The meaning is an abstract specification via which the intention is achieved. There are two components of meaning. The "X" component prescribes an object and the "predicate senses" prescribe the object's properties. Thus we see a certain thing as _____ (e.g. perceive an apple tree as blooming). There is also a background of meanings, a horizon of beliefs and conceptual schemes, presupposed by intentional acts.

So every perceptual act entails meanings that are abstract specifications. Unconscious wishes, too, are intentional acts, whose unacknowledged meanings specify desirable objects and states of affairs. The abstract specifications that we observe to link waking and dreaming worlds are to be understood, then, as intentional meanings.

1.8d The Causal Sequence of Dream World Formation

During waking, as we follow along our world line, we live certain meanings. We are intentional beings. Because I traumatically wake up with monumental sneezing during the night, and can't find the box of tissues, I happen to move my left arm a certain way, which turns out to be a movement of the left arm with three phases. So it just happens that I notice a three phase movement during waking. I use the meaning "three phase movement of the left arm." Later on, during REM sleep, my brain becomes activated through periodic brain stem mechanisms. Participatory to that activation, certain meanings that were operative during waking become re-operative, such as meaning a three phase movement of the left arm, which was emotionally significant because connected to a traumatic experience where I felt out of control. Once we reject the composition theory, then we are forced to the idea that the reoperative meanings have "something to do with" dream world formation. These abstract concepts "generate" (in a sense that requires unpacking) the concrete dream world and our life in it.

There is, however, a crucial difference between waking and dreaming meanings in their relations to their respective worlds. We recall that these worlds bear a family resemblance. Each world fulfills the meaning's specifications in its own way. The specification "three phase movement of the left arm" is equally fulfilled by my trying to find the tissues and by my operating the piece of medical equipment. But in the waking case the meaning was fulfilled "by reality;" while waking I actually did move my left arm in three distinct phases, so my meaning was not just an empty thought. In the dreaming case, however, "reality" is blocked out, and I have claimed that there are no memory traces that copy it. The dream world therefore must be spontaneously created by the meaning. The fulfillment of meaning during dreaming is *self-fulfilling*. *Meaning generates its own concrete fulfillment,* like the fully-armed Athena from the brow of Zeus. There is a movement from thought to perception. So when waking meanings become reoperative during dreaming (party to the general activation of REM sleep), they generate their own fulfillments in the form of a life-world.

We ordinarily do not consider meanings to have such power. They are considered to be empty thoughts unless filled by an autonomous "reality." But our investigation of dreams and rejection of the compositional theory of dream world formation forces the conclusion that abstract specifications have the extraordinary capacity to generate *de novo* the concrete life-world, especially under the condition of REM sleep. This conclusion diverges sharply from the causal theory of perception as Freud extended it to dreams.

We recall that for the traditional causal theory of waking perception, copies of sensory input are transformed by cognitive operations (Helmholtz's "unconscious inferences") so as to produce the world perceived. In Freud's causal theory of dream perception, there are additional stages. The end stage of the waking process is converted to mnemic copies that can be transformed by the dream work, under the aegis of unconscious wishful thought, to the dream world perceived. But on the present account, there are no mnemic copies to be transformed. Instead the perceived dream world is formed *de novo*.

1.8e Summary

The life-world of dreams is formed by intentional acts and their correlated abstract specifications. Waking intentionality becomes reoperative during REM sleep, and creates the dream world *de novo*. We form our dream lives through thought; our dream meanings generate their own concrete fulfillments.

1.9 THE CAPACITY FOR FORMATIVE CREATIVITY

1.9a Introduction

This chapter began with the question of creativity as seen in dreams. I critiqued Freud's conception of the dream work as creative like a *bricoleur,* compositing mnemic copies of past waking experiences into the dream experience, and also critiqued mechanical biological approaches that similarly relied on mnemic image composition. I suggested that the dream world derives from intentional meanings (Husserl's noematic Sinne) that were operative during waking and which became reoperative during REM sleep. A meaning made during a certain episode of waking (e.g. while monumentally sneezing, while discovering twins) generates its own fulfillment during dreaming, in conjunction with other relevant meanings, conscious and unconscious, operative at other past times and places. *The confluence of intentional acts and meanings generates the dream life.*

This extraordinary creativity has two distinct levels. There is first creativity in the sheer variety of unique life-worlds that dreaming constitutes *de novo*. The meanings co-operative in dreaming are typically a novel set, never before associated, and accordingly result in *creative variety*. Given the right meanings, any world from the set of all possible worlds might be produced.

But there is an even deeper level of creativity I shall call "formative" that should not be confused with creative variety. The point about the product of formative creativity is not its variety but its facticity, that there is any world at all, that our thought might produce its own fulfillment stretching there concretely before us. Usually we think of thought as empty, unfilled, abstract, so it is strange to conceive of thought as thinking up a world. Formative creativity is the power of Zeus.

Dreaming, then, reveals a fundamental formative creativity on which its creative variety depends. Dreaming is in this regard sharply distinguished from waking according to convention. We don't form the life-world of waking; this is just common sense. That world is already there, awaiting us, affording our unveilings of it. (Or in Heidegger, impatient with such dualism, we Da-seins are ek-static beings, self-surpassing, "always already outside ourselves in the world.") Of course, we *interpret* the world on the conventional view; what we find and how it looks depends on us. But the world is there in its own right, transcendent to us, and thereby not requiring any formative act on our part. In dreaming, however, we formatively create (generate, constitute) the very world and our life in it. Once we reject compositional theories of the dreaming life-world, formative creativity comes into focus. I next want to contrast formative creativity with "syntactical" creativity.

1.9b Syntactical Creativity

In syntactical creativity, the creative process arranges elements it is given in one configuration (even a random or arbitrary configuration, a *chaos*) into another configuration. Thus in formal mathematical systems axioms are transformed into theorems according to axiomatized rules of logic; symbol-elements are arranged in an initial string (formula) and then rearranged to another string (theorem). The idealized potter of Plato working at his or her element rearranges the homogeneous mound of clay to a bowl of clay according to the rule: Transform the clay in accordance with the *eidos,* the universal bowl. The very world is formed by the Platonic Demiurge (literally, craftsman) transforming the *chaos* given. The *bricoleur* collagist takes as elements found objects (*objets trouvés*) from divergent places and rearranges them by assembly into a work of art. The dream work of Freud takes as elements mnemic copies from divergent times of past waking experiences and rearranges (composits) them into dream worlds. All these are examples of syntactical creativity in that something elemental is given—elements ordered, disordered, or undifferentiated—and the elemental given is rearranged in a lawful fashion into something else.

1.9c The Process of Formative Creativity

It is clear that the theory of dream world formation developed above is not based on syntactical creativity. There are no elements given to be rearranged (*pace* the critique of Freud's compositional theory). The whole dreaming life-world is spontaneously and primarily formed as a whole, not as a secondary derivative of the waking life-world. Dreaming thought with its creative power somehow thinks up the dream world like Zeus thinks the fully armed Athena. In formative creativity, the whole product is produced all at once without benefit of initial elements.

The mechanism for accomplishing formative creativity will be left unremarked for now. Its consideration would take us far afield from the concerns of the present chapter, into the realm of machines. (The mechanism underlying the process of formative creativity will be discussed in 4.5.) But it is presently clear that with the failure of Freud's syntactically creative composition theory, there must be *some* process in which intentional acts are able to generate *de novo* their own fulfillment.

1.9d Formative Creativity in Lucid Dreaming

In the typical dream, a novel confluence of waking meanings reoperative during REM sleep generates the dreaming life-world. As considered thus far, this is a rather mechanical process. The general activation of REM sleep mechanically sweeps into operation those meanings most ready to be activated in virtue of their connection to unconscious wishes. In lucid dreaming, however, the dreamer decides which meanings are to be made operational so as to constitute the dream life. For example, LaBerge quotes a lucid dream of Saint-Denys who is riding a horse when he becomes lucid.

> I decide to gallop, I gallop; I decide to stop, I stop. Now here are two roads in front of me. The one on the right appears to plunge into a dense wood; the one on the left leads to some kind of ruined manor; I feel quite distinctly that I am free to turn either right or left, and so decide for myself whether I wish to produce images relating to the ruins or images relating to the wood. (LaBerge, 1985, p. 105)

Again, Van Eeden dreamt that he stood at a table on which were different objects. Being lucid, he decided to perform experiments.

> I began by trying to break glass, by beating it with a stone. I put a small goblet of glass on two stones and struck it with another stone. Yet it would not break. Then I took a fine claret-glass from the table and struck it with my fist, with all my might, at the same time reflecting how dangerous it would be to do this in waking life; yet the glass remained whole. But lo! When I looked at it again after some time, it was broken. (LaBerge, 1985, p. 30)

Thus the lucid dreamer just *thinks* the dream world he or she wants to live in, and lo, that world concretely appears.

The lucid dreamer's intention may be formed while dreaming, or be carried forward from the wake life. For an example of the latter, in LaBerge's work on sexual lucid dreams, the dreamer began to fly away from the laboratory on attaining lucidity.

> Continuing to fly, she found herself over a campus resembling both Oxford and Stanford. She flew through the cool evening air, free as a cloud, stopping now and then to admire the beautiful stone carvings on the walls. After a few minutes, however, she decided it was time to begin the experiment. Flying through an archway, she spotted a group of people—apparently visitors touring the campus. Swooping down to the group, she picked the first man within reach. She tapped him on the shoulder, and he came toward her as if knowing exactly what he was expected to do. (LaBerge, 1985, p. 83)

The dreamer quickly reaches a climax. Thus when the dreamer decides to start the experiment of having sexual activity, a life-world appears in which she has genuine sexual experience.

Now, the dream life that the lucid dreamer "consciously" thinks up could conceivably be a composition of memory traces *pace* Freud, but we have already rejected the composition theory above in relation to non-lucid dreams, and there is no compelling reason to resurrect it in the case of lucid dreams. Furthermore, the many lucid dreams *qua* dreams reported by LaBerge seem indistinguishable from non-lucid dreams *qua* dreams, and the composition theory is just as implausible in accounting for them. For the composition theory to hold in the sexual lucid dream just discussed, there would have to be memory traces of flying through the cool evening air and swooping down on a group of people, memory traces of tapping someone in a group on a college campus who approaches her expecting to make love, and memory traces of sexual activity, all of which would have to be effortlessly and immediately composited into an authentic and seamless dream life. The alternative theory of formative creativity explains lucid dreaming lives as constituted *de novo* by the lucid dreamer's deliberate thought, whereas non-lucid dream lives are constituted *de novo* by mechanically reoperative thoughts from waking. Thus the lucid dreamer has the power of Zeus!

1.9e Summary

The fundamental creativity of intentional meanings while dreaming is "formative," not "syntactical." In syntactical creation given elements are rearranged into the product, whereas in formative creation the product is spontaneously formed as a whole. Formative creativity is demonstrated by lucid dreaming.

1.10 REVIEW OF DREAM CREATIVITY

We are sentient in our dreams, and perceive a sometimes fantastic yet authentic life-world. Since our external senses are mostly closed down during sleep, the dreaming life-world must somehow be our own creation. For Freud that creation is second-hand, syntactical, relying on pre-existing memory traces of concrete waking experiences (e.g. riding a horse, hitting with the left arm), and also relying on a synthetic function that takes the hodge-podge of mnemic copies picked out by the unconscious dream thoughts and smoothly composits them into dreaming experiences. The resulting composites accordingly may be novel and bizarre, but nonetheless they inherit world-like properties. Whatever is truly creative in such a syntactical computer-like process comes under this synthetic function.

I have argued against Freud that the creativity of dreaming consciousness is first-hand, "de novo." The role of memory of concrete waking experiences is to provide something abstract (e.g. not a particular horse but the meaning of "horse," not a particular three-phase movement but the meaning of "three-phase movement"). Other operative meanings are related to both unconscious wishes and unconscious defenses against those wishes which were also active during waking. The life-world of dreams is generated by these active intentional meanings. Lucid dreams demonstrate the creative power of intentionality in remarkable fashion.

There is one striking apparent difference, however, between intentionality in waking and dreaming: In waking the meanings apparently specify the independent self-subsistent world, whereas in dreaming, the intentional meanings actually generate the world, spontaneously forming the world whole. This difference will be dissolved in chapter three.

We initially began this study of dream creativity with the thought that it might provide a window on the creativity of consciousness in general, since dreaming is a prime exemplar of creative consciousness. We discovered that dreaming consciousness is radically more creative and original than Freud thought, that we dream-think up sometimes stupendous worlds each night, that we are capable of formatively generating by purely abstract means concrete exemplifications of our meanings, like the thought of Zeus issues in the concrete Athena. We have the capacity to create the dreaming life-world formatively in its full authenticity. Since there is no sensory input while dreaming and no memory traces of concrete waking experiences to work with (per the critique of Freud), then it must be that the dreaming life-world is created *de novo*. Thus our dreams are first-hand creations, rather than put together from residues of waking life. *We have the capacity for infinite creativity;* at least while dreaming, we partake of the power of immanent Spirit, the infinite Godhead that creates the cosmos. In waking, we "contract away from infinity," as Wilber[34] says, and take a Heideggerian "fall" into a limited life-world.

But if we do have this extraordinary creative capacity while dreaming, then perhaps in waking we are much more creative than we know; that is, perhaps in waking as in dreaming . . . Indeed, we shall see that in the fundamental sense we are as creative in waking life as we are in the wildest of our dream lives. We do lose the capacity for creative variety during waking under the constraints of the sensory input absent during sleep, but formative creativity remains. Dreaming consciousness, then, with its formative creativity, will provide us a *via regia* to waking consciousness and the human condition.

Chapter Two

Dream
Phenomenology

> SOCRATES: *What evidence could be appealed*
> *to, supposing we were asked at this very*
> *moment whether we are asleep or awake?*
> THEAETETUS: *Indeed, Socrates, I do not see*
> *by what evidence it is to be proved; for the*
> *two conditions correspond in every cir-*
> *cumstance like exact counterparts.*
> —*Plato's* Theaetetus

2.1 INTRODUCTION

This chapter provides a bridge between the first and third chapters. The essential claim of the first chapter was that we spontaneously create the dreaming life-world *de novo* by abstract means. This creativity while dreaming is "formative;" the dream world is produced *de novo* rather than by a syntactical arranging of given elements. The third chapter just says the same thing for the waking life-world. The world we perceive during waking, the world "out there" in which we lead out waking lives, is not autonomous, not transcendent to our consciousness; we create *de novo* that commonsense world, too. The present bridging chapter sets the basis for equating dreaming to waking, by showing the *essential indiscernability of life-worlds in which we dwell while dreaming and waking.* Indiscernables demand the same explanation.

Now, there are some who would deny that there is any such thing as a dream life in a dream world anyway. Sartre in the existential tradition, Malcolm *pace* Wiggenstein, and Dennett the functionalist, all hold that there is no such thing as dream perception in which we might see, touch and think about a concrete world. For these writers, talk of a dreaming life-world is confused, meaningless, and plain wrong. The initial task of this chapter is to consider and reject these arguments that would deny authenticity to the life-world of dreams, giving it an essentially fictive status.

The subsequent task is to see if there are in fact cogent differences between dreaming and waking life-worlds or if, as Descartes held, there are "no certain indications" by which we may clearly distinguish dreaming from waking life.

> At this moment it does indeed seem to me that it is with eyes awake that I am looking at this paper; that this head which I move is not asleep, that it is deliberately and of set purpose that I extend my hand and perceive it . . . But in thinking over this I remind myself that on many occasions I have been deceived by similar illusions, and in dwelling on this reflection I see so manifestly that there are no certain indications by which we may clearly distinguish wakefulness from sleep that I am lost in astonishment. And my astonishment is such that it is almost capable of persuading me that I now dream. (Descartes, 1912, p. 145)

Leibniz similarly held,

> By no argument can it be demonstrated absolutely that bodies exist, nor is there anything to prevent certain well-ordered dreams from being the objects of our mind, which we judge to be true and which, because of their accord with each other are equivalent to truth so far as practice is concerned. (Leibniz, 1951, p. 603)

The received view is clearly that dreaming and waking life-worlds are indiscernable.

The method I adopt in comparing dreaming and waking life-worlds is to extend Husserl's phenomenological *epoche* to dreaming, which is to bracket our disbelief in the existence of the dream world, and then under the "double epoche" to consider dreaming and waking experience as we find it. Having adopted this method of the double epoche, there are several issues to consider that have been previously run together in the literature to the detriment of our understanding the relation between dreaming and waking life-worlds.

First, is the unreflective dream life *as lived* discernable from the unreflective wake life *as lived*, according to our waking recollection under the double epoche? That is, if we bracket our belief in the existence of the waking life and bracket our disbelief in the existence of the dream life, are these *lives-as-lived* discernable? The answer we shall come to is that these dream and wake lives as unreflectively lived are indiscernable. Second, can our waking reflection under the double epoche discern differences between dream and wake lives? The issue here is not these lives as we recall unreflectively living them, but what we can discern on studied reflection. (Note that reflection can confine its considerations to unreflective life as such or expand its inquiry to make observations outside of what the unreflective life might support, just as we might adopt an arithmetic or metamathematical perspective on a formalized calculus.) We shall find that reflection not confined to life-as-lived is able to distinguish dream and wake lives. This third question then comes into focus: Does the discernability of dreaming and waking lives to waking reflection undermine their indiscernability as lives lived? The answer here is that the differences reflection notes are not fundamental but related to sensory functions, which are highly restricted in sleep and open during waking. The dream life is like the wake life, except that there is no flowing array of sensory stimulation available to modulate it. *As lived,* the dream life is an authentic life, but reflection reveals that it is a peculiar unmodulated life because of the sensory restriction.

2.2 THE DENIAL OF DREAM PERCEPTION

Philosophers have been interested in dreams since antiquity. Aristotle considered both sleep and dreams at some length.[1] Descartes, in his quest for certainty, was forced to face the compelling illusion of dreams, and Hobbes said "the difficulty in distinguishing the waking state from dreams is a matter of common observation . . . of ancient lore" going back to the Greek philosophers.[2] This position is mainstream. Dennett says that Aristotle, Descartes, Kant, Russell, Moore and Freud all accept

> the received view . . . that dreams consist of sensations, thoughts, impressions, and so forth, usually composed into coherent narratives or adventures, occurring somehow in awareness or consciousness, though in some sense or way the dreamer is *uncon*scious during the episode. (Dennett, 1978, p. 129)

The contemporary denial by some philosophers that we ever perceive a life-world while dreaming challenges in a fundamental way the present thesis that there is a dreaming life-world indiscernable from the life-world of waking, and so I shall focus on the arguments against dream experience.

The issue has actually already been decided by laboratory research on lucid dreaming.[3] (See 1.1 and 1.9d above.) Lucid dreamers can signal their awareness of dreaming while the EEG shows the pattern of REM sleep, and through prearranged signals indicate the dream content. Lucid dreamers can correctly estimate elapsed time. They can breathe rapidly or hold their breath while dreaming, and this corresponds to objective measurement of their respiration. They can sing or count, and their right and left brains are respectively activated, just as in waking.

The empirical evidence is thus strong that dreams are something more than reports on awakening, i.e. there is good evidence that the reports actually refer to dream experiences. In lucid dreaming there is no temporal gap between dream and dream report, which critical philosophers might seize on. The lucid dreamer's report—sent through eye movements, since the other musculature is inhibited during REM sleep—coincides with the dream experience, and the report can be validated against objective physiological recording. Philosophical arguments against dream experience are still worth rebutting, however, not so much for the bottom line but for the key issues exposed as the rebuttal is developed. The remainder of 2.2, however, is not essential to my argument.

2.2a Sartre

In *The Psychology of Imagination* (1940) Sartre presents the following argument denying that there is dreaming perception of a life-world. He points out that reflective consciousness does not occur for the dreamer, but in fact disrupts the dream.

> ... the position of existence of the dreamer cannot be likened to that person who is awake, because the reflective consciousness, in the one case, destroys the dream, by the very fact that it presents it for what it is, whereas in the case of perception reflective consciousness confirms and reinforces the perception itself. (Sartre, 1940, p. 233)

And so,

> To affirm that I perceive is to deny that I am dreaming ...
> (p. 235)
> ... the dream consciousness is completely deprived of the faculty of perceiving. It does not perceive, nor does it seek to perceive, nor can it even conceive what a perception is. (p. 239)

Nevertheless, the fact remains that we unreflectively encounter a dream world in a way that at times—in well developed cases—can be indistinguishable from ways that we unreflectively encounter the wake world. As Malcolm says, " ... sometimes a man may wake up with the impression that certain incidents occurred and may be in doubt as to whether those incidents belonged to a dream or to reality."[4] So vivid are some dream experiences that we have to "figure out" that they are "only dreams."

For example, I once had similar nightmares several times over a few years. I dreamt on each occasion that I had killed someone, who was walled up in my home. I was anguished in these dreams that my grisly deed would come out. So vivid were these dream nightmares that on awakening I was uncertain for a time whether or not I had in fact killed someone; I had to reason through that I was not a murderer. What was especially difficult was that the repetitive nature of the dream experience gave the dream murder a temporal history. On awakening from the later episodes, as I lay fearfully trying to convince myself that I hadn't "really" killed someone, my deed stretched into a remembered past, even to the anguish relating to what had "really" happened. (What I had "killed" and "walled off," I think, was my authenticity and resoluteness during the period when I first was existentially confronted with my own death; my fearful anguish was over the finiteness of my being. My psychoanalytic colleagues will of course suggest a different interpretation.) So Sartre's argument against dream experience comes up against compelling personal experience. As Farber says, "That which is seen cannot be explained away, and is the final standard in all truly philosophical thought."

Even if we grant Sartre's point that we do not reflect in dreams that we are dreaming (putting aside for now lucid dreams in which the dreamer notes that he or she is dreaming), this does not bear upon our perception of a dream world which is prereflective. Reflection, as Merleau-Ponty points out, should not lose sight of its own beginning. On reflecting, my reflection bears upon an unreflective experience as lived, and it is just this unreflective experience of a world which is at times indistinguishable across waking and dreaming. So we may reflect in waking on either unreflective waking or unreflective dreaming experience as lived.

The present point is not whether there are "certain indications" by means of which reflective reason can distinguish waking from dreaming life-worlds. Instead the point is that the life-world while dreaming "looks like" an authentic world and is "taken" to be an authentic world, no matter what reason later says about this perception. The present concern is thus with issues surrounding pre-reflective perceptual experience, not with issues of perceptual experience reflected upon or of skepticism.

2.2b Malcolm

Malcolm's argument is coherent with Sartre's. He observes,

Many philosophers and psychologists have thought that when one dreams one reasons, judges, imagines, has sense-impressions, and so on, while asleep. They have thought that to dream is to do those acts or have those experiences in the *same* sense that people do them or have them when awake. There may be differences in degree of clarity, intensity or coherence, but that is all. (Malcolm, 1959, p. 51)

It is this position that Malcolm seeks to deny. His argument is cunning and difficult to get hold of, so I shall quote him extensively.

Malcolm distinguishes between sleeping and waking. One can neither assert nor judge nor wonder nor doubt that he is asleep, because these acts are prima facie evidence that one is *not* asleep. (Again, Malcolm is talking of non-lucid dreams.) The claim "I am asleep" thus has no sense for Malcolm, because it cannot be verified. But there is verification for the claim that I have dreamt, and that verification is just the dream telling on awakening. The dream report, however, does *not* imply that there was any dream perception of a life-world while asleep.

If after waking from sleep a child tells us that he saw and did and thought various things, none of which could be true, and if his relation of these incidents has spontaneity and no appearance of invention, then we may say to him 'It was a dream'. We do not question whether he really had a dream or if it merely seems to him that he did. (Malcolm, 1959, p. 55)

Talk of dreams is just part of a "language-game."

If we object to Malcolm that we in fact *remember* the dream experience, he retorts that 'remember' has a special use in the language-game of dreams. A waking memory after all can be verified as right or wrong.

But when I speak of 'remembering' a dream there is nothing outside of my account of the dream ... to determine that my account is right or wrong ... That something is implausible or impossible does not go to show that I did not dream it. In a dream I can do the impossible in every sense of the word. I can climb Everest without oxygen and I can square the circle. Since nothing counts as determining that my memory of my dream is right or wrong, what sense can the word 'memory' have here? (Malcolm, 1959, p. 57)

So there is no criterion for determining if any dream experience actually occurred; there is only the dream telling.

> ... in our daily discourse about dreams what we take as determining beyond question that a man dreamt is that in sincerity he should tell a dream or say he had one. (Malcolm, 1959, p. 59)

Dennett makes the same point pithily.

> If asked what it is like to dream one *ought* to say (because it would be the truth): "It is not like anything. I go to sleep and when I wake up I find I have a tale to tell, a 'recollection' as it were." (Dennett, 1978, p. 139)

Dream tellings, then, do not validate dream experience for Malcolm and Dennett.

The dream is actually *inferred* according to Malcolm. There is no question that we have the "impression" that certain dream events occurred, that they "seem" to occur. But the issue is "whether your impression corresponds with reality, and to discover that it does not is to discover that you had a dream."[5] So when pushed about the validity of our dream experience, we must resort to inference.

> To find out one dreamt the incident is to find out that the impression one had on waking is false ... If we know that it is impossible for a certain thing to have occurred then the waking impression that it occurred is false, and we know therefore that one dreamt the impossible thing. (Malcolm, 1959, ps. 64–65)

A dream telling, then, does not imply that the dreamer was aware of dream experiences while asleep.

> When he says 'I dream so and so' he implies, first, that it seemed to him on waking up as if the so and so had occurred and, second, that the so and so did not occur. There is simply no place here for an implication or assumption that he was aware of anything at all while asleep. (Malcolm, 1959, p. 66)

Malcolm's bottom line is thus simply that it is impossible to verify that there are dream lives to which dream tellings allude, and so a dream life is senseless and superfluous.

> One tells a dream under the influence of an impression—*as if* one was faithfully recalling events that one witnessed. Telling a dream is undoubtedly a queer phenomenon. (Malcolm, 1959, p. 86)

He acknowledges the protest that the phenomenon is not queer at all, the protest that the most likely explanation of our *seeming* to recall a dream life is that we actually did *have* such a life. But here he quotes Wittgenstein to the effect that "it is an important thing in philosophy to know when to *stop.*"[6]

> If we cease to ask *why* it is that sometimes when people wake up they relate stories in the past tense under the influence of an impression, then we will see dream-telling as it is—a remarkable human phenomenon, a part of the natural history of man, something *given*, the foundation for the concept of dreaming. (Malcolm, 1959, p. 87)

There is a lot more to Malcolm's argument, but I think this is the main thread to it.

Against Malcolm, note that he fully concedes the indiscernability between waking life and dream-tellings; an inference is required to distinguish the dream life, so indiscernable is it from the wake life. Now, we can easily distinguish in waking between a fictitious story about ourselves and a story about something we actually witnessed. I could tell you a story about my taking a rocket trip to the moon yesterday or a story of plugging away at this typewriter, but I know immediately and without inference which I actually witnessed. The one is "empty" and the other "filled." Given this capacity, why should we be confused about whether our dream stories are empty or filled by past lives? In fact, we are not confused at all. We know non-inferentially our dream stories to be filled, and Malcolm concedes, indiscernably so from how our wake stories are filled, "*as if* one was faithfully recalling events that one witnessed."[7]

So we know what it is (as "part of the natural history of man") for a story to be filled—we recall the filling—and we know that our dream story is filled—we recall the dream filling—and our dream recallings and the dream fillings are indiscernable from our waking recallings and fillings. We must be given extremely good grounds, then, if we are to swallow that we just are mistaken in the dream case—and instead of good grounds Malcolm talks of a "queer phenomenon" and opines that philosophers needs to know when to stop asking questions! Malcolm's argument is thus *ad hoc*, evasive and prima facie implausible; his only ground against a dream life turns out to be an allegiance to Wittgenstein.[8]

It must be conceded I think, that there are *some* dream stories which are unfilled, purely cognitive dreams. Not every dream that we might have is perceptually developed; many are wholly thought-like. These purely cognitive dreams are equivalent to empty stories.

We must grant good faith to Sartre (and to Dennett) that their dream stories in fact are never filled, but Malcolm's dreams are filled, as shown by his admitting indiscernability. Presumably there are some people whose dream stories are *always* empty—brilliantly cognitive people, perhaps—and such people would be honestly led to claim that dream tellings do not make reference to any concrete dream life while asleep. But the fact remains that for most of us—including Plato, Descartes, Leibniz, Kant, Russell, Moore, and Freud—there are at least some dream stories that are vividly filled.

My point here is admittedly *ad hominem*, but I think justifiably so. When people differ in good faith about something so basic as whether or not they perceive a dreaming life-world, the simplest explanation is that the people have different capabilities.[9] Since most of us have some cognitive dreams, it is not surprising that some of us might have only cognitive dreams, and accordingly mistakenly find any alleged indiscernability of dreaming and waking life-worlds to be wrong.

2.2c Dennett

Dennett's argument against dream experience basically follows Malcolm, but he adds a novel argument to the effect that dream time can be long while clock time is short, so the dream time could not have been experienced.[10] In support of this view, Dennett recounts this dream.

> In a recent dream of mine I searched long and far for a neighbor's goat; when at last I found her she bleated *baa-a-a*—and I awoke to find her bleat merging perfectly with the buzz of an electric alarm clock I had not used or heard for months. (Dennett, 1978, p. 135)

Since the dream went on and on while the alarm that presumably stimulated the dream buzzed only briefly, Dennett thinks that the desperate defender of dream experience is forced to assume "precognition." The dreamer must somehow have *foreseen* that the alarm would be going off just when it did, and the dream story prepared for the precognized event of the alarm. This is of course implausible.

Since a dream life of "searching far and wide" could not be compressed into the relatively few seconds the alarm was ringing, Dennett favors instead a "cassette theory" in explaining the dream. In this theory dream narratives are composed directly into memory banks.

> ... perhaps there is a "library" in the brain of undreamed [i.e. never experienced] dreams with various indexed endings, and the bang or bump or buzz has the effect of retrieving an appropriate dream and inserting it, cassette-like, in the memory mechanism. (Dennett, 1978, p. 136, brackets added)

On waking this "cassette" is played back and the person mistakenly believes that he or she had a dream experience. Dennett doesn't tell us where the "library" of undreamed dreams come from, but Freud has a suggestion.

Freud had discussed exactly this kind of dream in *The Interpretation of Dreams* and had come to a similar explanation. Freud considered a dream of Maury's in which Maury had a long and elaborate experience set at the time of the French Revolution. Maury's dream ended with his being guillotined. He awoke to find the top of the bed had fallen down and hit him on the neck just where the guillotine struck! Freud suggests[11] that Maury had had waking fantasies of the French Revolution "stored up ready-made in his memory for many years" and the dream "experience" was actually a recollection of the past fantasies. So Dennett's "library of undreamed dreams" comes from waking fantasy, according to Freud.

Freud similarly discussed a dream of the playwright Casimir Bonjour.[12] Bonjour fell asleep just as a play of his began on opening night. He went through all five acts and observed the audience's emotions during the different scenes. At the end his name was shouted and there was loud applause. He awoke to find only the first few lines of the first scene had been performed. Freud again suggests that Bonjour's waking fantasy of his play's reception was stored in memory and recalled on awakening. Thus Freud agrees with Dennett that for this type of dream, there was actually no dream experience. Of course, Dennett thinks there is *never* any such thing as dream experience, and here Freud would not agree, considering such dreams to be special cases.

Dennett also mentions two other possible explanations of his dream. Perhaps such dreams are

> composed and presented *very fast* in the interval between bang, bump or buzz and full consciousness, with some short delay system postponing the full "perception" of the noise in the dream until the presentation of the narrative is ready for it. (Dennett, 1978, p. 136)

Or perhaps such dreams are composed, presented and recorded backwards and then remembered forwards. But he thinks that these explanations are inconsistent with there being any such things as experiences while dreaming; the dream, after all, does not run fast like a twenties movie.[13] So there are no dream experiences for Dennett, only recollections on waking.

Now, given the creativity of dreaming argued for in chapter one, we would expect that the dream time is constituted *de novo* along with everything else in dreams. Indeed, if we look at time in a Heideggerian way, even waking time is a creation. For Heidegger, "Temporality temporalizes itself" as the fundamental process of the human being's (Dasein's) existence.[14] It would not be surprising if dreaming Dasein also supported the process of Temporality temporalizing itself.

Heidegger's idea seems to be that there is an autochthonous (primordial, original) *now* that is "stretched" (given dimensionality) in virtue of the temporalizing process. There are three ways of stretching the original now, only two of which presently concern us. The first is now as duration. What we mean by now-duration varies.

> When any one of us says "now" we all understand this now, even though each of us perhaps dates this now by starting from a different thing or event: "now, when the professor is speaking," "now when the students are writing," or "now, in the morning," "now, towards the end of the semester." (Heidegger, 1927, p. 264)

This now-as-stretched has a functional significance (a "time to . . . ") and a datability (a "time when . . . "). Daseins can also agree on a public now, standardized by the movement of clocks. It should be noted that the duration of the now has a lower limit; we cannot experience a now of too brief a duration, a now less than an *augenblick* (eyeblink). This lower limit is William James' "specious present," and is on the order of tenths of a second. The second stretch of now is that the now always expects the future and retains the past, so that we should properly speak of now, then, and at-the-time. So the original now is stretched to a duration determined by our functionalities and datings, and is also stretched to past and future in terms of retentions and expectations.

Similarly, there is a dream now stretched as a "time to . . . " and a "time when . . . ", and also stretched by retention and expectation. The dream time is whatever dreaming Temporality temporalizes. Let us apply this notion to Dennett's dream.

The dreaming Dennett (whose metaphor I shall take rather literally, to make my point) experiences a now where he is looking far, a now where he is looking wide, and a now where he finds the goat. In the now of looking far he expects to find the goat, and in the now of looking wide he retains looking far and expects to find the goat, and in the now of finding the goat ("at last") he retains looking both far and wide.

So the dream time comprises a sequence of variously stretched now durations (looking far, looking wide), each stretched to then and at-the-time. Suppose Dennett's buzzer is on 6 seconds before he hears it. Then assuming (for ease of calculation) the lower limit of the now is .6 seconds, the dreaming Dennett might have had up to 10 nows (now, looking far here; now, looking far there; now, looking wide over there . . .), while a waking observer would have had only one now (now, when the buzzer is buzzing).

My account of dream time still may seem implausible. Suppose each scene in the five acts of Bonjour's play was a dream now lasting .6 seconds on the non-dream clock, a now retentive of past scenes and expectant of future scenes. How does a 6 minute scene get packed in .6 seconds?

What must be appreciated here is that *per impossible* in the absence of Temporality temporalizing itself, the order of world configurations comprising the scene would have *no time at all*. Time would return to the original now which is without dimensionality (unstretched); there would be a before and after that determines order, but not an earlier and later. The sequence of world configurations while dreaming may be run off faster *or* slower than comparable world configurations while waking, since the former is unanchored to the real world and freely created. But the time of the sequence of dream world configurations is whatever time dreaming Temporality temporalizes, in accordance with the viscissitudes of the dream work (whether understood in Freudian, Jungian or Daseinsanalytic ways).

There is one crucial difference between waking and dreaming time. In waking, temporality is yoked to movements in the transcendent world, standardized by clocks, the public now. However each Dasein's now happens to be stretched, its succession of now-durations, and its thens and at-the-times, are mappable onto clock time. In dreaming, temporality is typically disengaged from the transcendent world with its clocks and comes under the aegis of the dream work. The dream time is a spontaneous production of dreaming Dasein, of Temporality temporalizing itself while dreaming.

The exception to the disengagement of dream temporality from the transcendent world is when a sharp stimulus during REM sleep—an alarm buzzing or the bed top falling—intrudes upon the dream. The dream then incorporates the stimulus into the dream world for a time, until the dreamer awakens. (Note the transition where Dennett simultaneously hears *baa-a-a* and buzzer.) Freud thought the most basic wish expressed in the dream is the wish to go on sleeping. The dream attempts to incorporate the stimulus—converts buzz to *baa-a-a*—so as to continue sleeping. Indeed, Dennett's dream is very typical of alarm clock dreams, which often seem especially prolonged. (He searched "far and wide" and found the goat "at last.") Thus dream temporality stretches to accommodate the wish to go on sleeping; in general, dreaming temporality is determined by wishes, rather than the claims of transcendent clocks that anchor waking temporality.

So that Dennett's dream experience lasted a long time while the clock alarm that provoked it lasted only a short time does not count against dream experience. The dream has its own experienced time—an authentic time continuously created *de novo*—notwithstanding what the clocks of waking show.

2.2d Summary

I have argued at length against those who would deny a life-world to dreaming, and have concluded that their position is without merit. Having admitted a dreaming life-world, we now can examine more closely the claim that dreaming and waking life-worlds are essentially indiscernable. A method is required for this investigation. I turn to Husserl's *epoche,* which is a basic phenomenological procedure, and extend it to dreams.

2.3 The Method of the Dream *Epoche*

In the epoche, existence is bracketed; no position is taken either for or against factual existence. Things still appear to exist, but this existence is taken as pure phenomenon. Note that in accomplishing the epoche, it is far easier to bracket the exceptional belief that things do not exist than it is to bracket the belief that things do exist, for in the natural standpoint we unquestioningly accept that things exist. The epoche, then, is directed towards existential belief.

The world experienced in this reflectively grasped life goes on being for me (in a certain manner) "experienced" as before, and with just the content it has at any particular time. It goes on appearing, as it appeared before; the only difference is that I, as reflecting philosophically, no longer keep in effect (no longer accept) the natural believing in existence involved in experiencing the world—though that believing too is still there and grasped by my noticing regard. (Husserl, 1913, p. 19)

I interpret the epoche as follows.

Husserl wants to look at conscious being without encumbrance by any belief. This is an essentially Cartesian quest, a quest for absolute, "apodictic" certainty, for a blessed freedom from doubt, as foundation on which to erect philosophy. So he jettisons his natural belief in the existence of his life-world, and takes the life-world just as he finds it, as pure phenomenon, as appearance. Thus reflection views unreflective common sense experience dispassionately, without even belief in the life-world's existence. Of course, one of the characteristics that phenomenological reflection finds is our belief in the world and our life in it, but this is just a belief to be bracketed.

Now, there are two forms of conscious being, according to the present discussion, waking and dreaming. Each form of concious being unreflectively believes in the existence of its life-world. As we reflect on unreflective waking being, we bracket our natural belief (and unnatural disbelief) in the life-world's existence. We note the belief, but remain uncommitted, under the waking epoche. As we reflect on unreflective dreaming being, we bracket our natural *dis*belief (and unnatural belief) in the dreaming life-world's existence. All beliefs must go under the epoche!

The reason Husserl did not extend his epoche to dreams, I think, is that he did not radically enough uproot his beliefs. He let go his natural belief in the existence of the waking life-world, but kept the natural attitude's belief in the non-existence of the dreaming life-world. My proposal to extend the epoche to dreams, then, is to bracket a belief that has full parity with our waking belief in the world's existence, viz. the unreflective near universal belief in the dream world's non-existence (just the belief that Malcolm so confidently espouses). But this is only to make thoroughly radical the phenomenological epoche.

The double epoche thus makes possible an unbiased approach to the issue of the indiscernability of dreaming and waking life-worlds. We bracket our natural beliefs in the waking life-world's existence and the dreaming life-world's nonexistence, and compare what we find. The issue is, adopting the dream epoche, whether or not there are essential differences between the life-worlds of dreaming and waking.

2.4 INDISCERNABLE DREAMING AND WAKING LIFE-WORLDS AS UNREFLECTIVELY ENCOUNTERED

The influence of the dream epoche is salutary, I think, because it makes us look at our dream life in a fresh way. Rather than regarding our dream life as illusory and thereby depreciating it, we take it as a life we lead. The dream life is an unreflective life, like our ordinary, non-philosophical, unreflective wake life. In waking, we also may reflect philosophically upon our unreflective dream life and unreflective wake life.

In living our dream life, it certainly seems as authentic as our wake life. The world seems real. Our actions in it seem actual. We have thoughts. We feel and care about what happens, just as in the wake life. We have purposes, some gratified and others frustrated. But there appear to be some differences.

The dream life is often hazy, shadowy, poorly developed and only sometimes as vivid as the wake life. The dream life often is bizarre and transparently has symbolic meanings. It is exceptionally "single-minded," and in some regards "isolated" from the wake life, as Recht-schaffen says. But these peculiarities are not available to the dream life as lived.

Our dream life in a hazy dream just seems like a hazy life. If bizarre, then that is just the way the world happens to be right then. Sometimes we may say to ourself while dreaming, "Gee, this is bizarre" and even add, "It's only a dream," but nevertheless we remain "thrown" (Heidegger) in the dreaming life-world, however bizarre it may be. The dream may have symbolic meanings, but the dreamer rarely attempts an interpretation while dreaming. "What you see is what you get," insofar as the unreflective dreamer is concerned. (There is no Ricoeurian "hermeneutics of suspicion" for the dreamer.) We do not typically observe while dreaming that we are being single-minded, but we do typically feel quite "caught up" in our dreaming life-world; we are somehow "rapt." We do not typically note the isolation of the dream life from some of the wake life (e.g. that we are "actually" in our bed asleep). The dream life has its own past too, which mainly merges with our waking past. We are still the same person by and large in our dream life, even though we may do some funny things.

The unreflective dream life as lived and the unreflective wake life as lived are thus indiscernable, so indiscernable that the waking Descartes by the fire wonders if he may be deceived. The dream life is just a part of our unreflective life where we happen to be especially caught up, may be bizarrely "thrown," and are much too occupied to be interested in what it all really means, although such things happen in the unreflective wake life too. It is all the same life . . . Since the life-worlds of dreaming and waking are indiscernable *as unreflectively lived,* the distinctions evident to waking studied reflection become of great importance, for they might undermine the patent indiscernability.

2.5 The 'Single-Mindedness' of Dreams

Rechtschaffen has provided a stimulating phenomenological discussion of the psychological properties that distinguish dreaming from waking to studied reflection. He suggests that what is most distinctive of dreaming is its "singlemindedness."

> By the "single-mindedness" of dreams, I mean the strong tendency for a single train of related thoughts and images to persist over extended periods without disruption or competition from other simultaneous thoughts and images. (Rechtschaffen, 1978, p. 97)

We are fascinated with the dream world and our life in it.

This peculiar single-mindedness of dreams can be easily demonstrated. Last night I dreamt I was in a hotel making love with a young woman, and my wife walked in. I tried to hide, but my companion called out to her and I was discovered. I felt very upset, and expected the worst, but my wife was quite understanding. She said that she was interested in a certain man, but I felt relieved, thinking to myself that the man is gay.

Now, this dream experience of behaving, perceiving, feeling, expecting and thinking seemed entirely authentic (although in this dream somehow less bright, hazier, less vivid than waking experience), and in the dream I did not question it. I did not say to myself, while dreaming, "Now wait a minute. When you went to sleep you were with your wife and children in a cabin in the woods. What are you doing in a hotel with this honey?" This is what Rechtschaffen calls the "isolation" of dreams; they are essentially discontinous with waking life. It is not that my dream had no past, but only that it did not take into account my sleeping circumstances. In earlier scenes of the dream I was at an academic meeting where I comported myself academically. My dream past was by and large confined to the meeting, with an ill-defined sense of myself as having an academic history. I was single-mindedly caught up with the events of this meeting throughout the dream, and this dream life had its own academic past, quite isolated from my immediate waking past but quite consonant with my general past.

In this typically single-minded dream I am situated within a horizon of meanings, situated "at an academic meeting," situated sexually, situated within a certain relationship with my wife. All of these ways of being situated are temporalized, so that the marital relationship has a past and a future (I expect the worst based on the past) and a present (I am given understanding). The world that I encounter within this horizon is full, complete, not calling itself into question as possibly illusory, any more than my current world of composing and typing this chapter calls itself into question. My dream Being constitutes its own past, present and future, just as does my waking Being, as we saw in the discussion of Dennett's dream. There is some overlap between dream time and wake time. In the dream time I am a person who has lived an academic life that I have actually lived during waking, but I am not the person who has been living in the woods. (The dream horizon does not include an "in the woods" situatedness.)

I think Rechtschaffen's valuable discussion of the single-mindedness of dreams is ultimately misleading, however. He distinguishes sharply between waking reflectiveness and what he considers dreaming nonreflectivemess as follows.

Waking consciousness generally contains at least two prevalent streams. One stream contains "voluntary" mental productions, thoughts and images that "pop" into our heads, and sense impressions. The other is a reflective or evaluative stream which seemingly monitors the first and places it in some perspective. The reflective stream seems to judge whether the thoughts or images are integral to the mental task of the moment or irrelevant intrusions from a separate part of our minds—whether the thoughts are deliberate, voluntary mental productions, or spontaneous, uncontrolled thoughts—whether the images come to us from the external world or from within. In dreams, the reflective stream of consciousness is drastically attentuated. While we are dreaming, we are usually unaware that we are lying in bed, unaware that the images before us are hallucinatory, and unaware that we are dreaming. (Rechtschaffen, 1978, p. 98)

Reflection while dreaming is not relevant to our "actual" conditions—that we are "actually" lying in bed—but to our dream conditions. In my dream I surely reflected upon my condition of being in bed, caught *flagrante delicto! Dream reflection takes place within the dream horizon,* and except for those capable of lucid dreaming or the occasional dream reassurance "this is only a dream," the dream horizon does not situate us for any sleep condition. Rechtschaffen thinks we ought to evaluate while dreaming that the dream is a mere hallucination, like we distinguish having "peculiar thoughts and images dozens of times a day"[15] that intrude irrelevantly upon us from having "images come to us from the external world" that are "integral to the mental task of the moment."[16] He finds our failure to do so unreflective. But the comparision is not apt. The dream thoughts and images in no way irrelevantly intrude upon us but seem to come from the external world and be integral to the task at hand, just as in waking. Rechtschaffen's point reduces to the observation that while dreaming we do not reflect on our waking situation, which does not mean we are always unreflective while dreaming, only that our reflection occurs within the dreaming rather than the waking horizon.

The dream characteristics Rechtschaffen points to can be subsumed under the peculiar *persistence of the dream horizon,* which may or may not be associated with reflection within that horizon. Recall he defines singlemindedness as "the strong tendency for a single train of related thoughts and images to persist over extended periods without disruption or competition from other simultaneous thoughts and images;"[17] the "single train" here is determined by the persisting dream horizon. Another dream characteristic, Rechtschaffen says, is the lack of "imagination" in the sense of "the capacity to conjure up images and thoughts which may occupy consciousness simultaneously or near simultaneously with another stream of thoughts and images."[18] Dream reports do not take the form, " 'Well I was dreaming of such and such, but as I was dreaming this I was imagining a different scene which was completely unrelated.' "[19] I think what Rechtschaffen points to here is that in waking we can simultaneously or near simultaneously maintain two horizons, while in dreaming there tends to be but one persistent horizon. When the horizon shifts (which probably tends to happen together with the gross body movements that punctuate REM sleep), it does so abruptly, and we say in reporting the dream, "Suddenly I found myself . . . ". The "thematic coherence" of dreams—that "dreams do tend to take the form of a story"[20] and tell one story at a time—again reflects the persistence of the dream horizon.

Finally, the characteristic that dreams are poorly recalled can also be attributed to the persisting dream horizon. Rechtschaffen observes,

> We can now speculatively infer that one reason for the massive forgetting of dreams is that the conditions which limit dreaming consciousness to a single thought stream also limit the capacity to simultaneously adopt a set for remembering that thought stream, i.e., typically we cannot or do not say to ourselves during the dream, "I must remember this." (Rechtschaffen, 1978, p. 103)

That is, one reason we tend not to remember dreams is because the persisting dream horizon does not support flagging the experience for remembering.

So these characteristics of dreaming, which on studied reflection are distinguishable from waking, point to a horizon more persisting than that of waking, where our horizons shift more fluidly. But this is only to be expected, given the special conditions of sleep. During waking, the horizon is in part determined by what the world affords. Even if it is so that we only perceive what we are prepared to perceive in virtue of our horizon, what is picked up from the world in turn shifts the further development of the horizon. *Sensory input modulates the waking horizon.* During sleep there is typically nothing picked up from the world and so the horizon is not shifted by the input flux, but persists. *In the absence of input during sleep there is a certain inertia to the dream horizon.*

Considering this account of dream horizon persistence more deeply, we note that those aspects of the waking horizon that *are* relatively immune to sensory input from the world are in fact just as persistent as the dream horizon. I mean here the conventional beliefs of Heidegger's *das Man*, life strategies, unconscious wishes, and the like that are maintained more or less single-mindedly through the viscissitudes of our input flux as we follow along our world line. *Das Man* holds our waking life every bit as rapt as we are in our dream life! So the single-mindedness and isolation of dreams that on reflection distinguish dreaming from waking are a function of the sensory conditions of sleep that promote persistence of the dream horizon, compared to the more fluid wake horizon. When in waking it happens that our horizon persists—when completely absorbed in what is going on—then dreaming and waking are indiscernable.

2.6 THE BIZARRENESS AND SYMBOLIC NATURE OF DREAMS

Rechtschaffen mentions another possible reflective distinction between dreaming and waking in his opening statement, but does not develop it.

> The most noted psychological properties of dreams, their bizarreness and their meaningfulness or symbolic value, are neither unique to nor even remarkably distinctive of dreaming. (Rechtschaffen, 1978, p. 97)

But then he tempers this judgment.

> My intent here is not to begrudge the attention to bizarreness and meaning; many dreams are more bizarre and symbolic than most waking thought. Rather, I do want to contrast this attention to the scant notice given to . . . the "single-mindedness" of dreams. (Rechtschaffen, 1978, p. 97)

I think we should take seriously the bizarreness of some dreams and the symbolic meanings of most dreams as distinguishing characteristics. Here again, we can attribute these characteristics to the dream horizon under the special conditions of sleep.

Let us recall the peculiar conditions of sleep (so perspicuously discussed by Freud), where the sensory mechanisms are by and large shut down (although they remain selectively open, as when mother quickly awakens to the child calling "mama"). In the dreaming state, concepts are relatively "unbridled." Sensory input bridles waking conceivings; if our waking conceivings were not modulated by informational properties of our surrounding energy sea, then we would quickly become "out of sync" with our surroundings—and as a species extinct. But the set of concepts activated during REM sleep are not so constrained. They flourish according to their own tendencies, unchecked by what the energy sea affords, subject only to defenses that are themselves related to the wishful concepts. The concepts operational during dreaming are accordingly a bizarre set. They have nothing to adapt to biologically, because they have no direct behavioral consequences. The concepts activated in this unbridled way are importantly "unconscious," as Freud was the first to see.

Freud's idea was that certain concepts are just always operational, waking or sleeping, whatever the input flux. These concepts are integral to wishes that we do not acknowledge in waking, indeed struggle against acknowledging. Put in terms of intentionality (*pace* Searle), the dreaming intentional state comprises a type of intention (wishing) and an intentional content (specification of the "object" that would satisfy the wish-intention). For waking intentional states, when the input flux meets the specifications of certain intentional contents within the whole network of inter-related specifications, we say that certain information has been "picked up." What is less often emphasized is that there is a two-way process going on here. The information of the input flux is not only picked up by the intentional content but input also "picks out" the intentional contents that it matches, and sustains and enhances the intentional content picked out. These intentional contents matched achieve a special status with respect to the comprehensive whole of intentional contents in which the matched content is embedded. For dreaming intentional states, however, there is no input to adjudicate between intentional contents, which are left to their own inherent powers. Those most powerful in their own right, it was Freud's genius to see, were the intentional contents of unconscious wishes, especially childhood wishes, especially childhood wishes related to oral, anal and genital bodily zones.

Now, to finish up this translation of Freudian theory into intentional (Searlean) terms, the set of dream intentional contents generates life-worlds that satisfy the intentional content's abstract specifications ("conditions of satisfaction"). This appears to contrast with waking intentional contents that are satisfied by an autonomous life-world. Those unconscious concepts (the wishful dream-thoughts), whose expression during waking is much muted due to sensory modulation of operational concepts, come into their own during sleeping. They bring along with them adventitiously associated concepts. (For example, in Freud's famous dream of the botanical monograph,[21] he just happened to see a botanical monograph on Cyclamen in the window of a bookshop on the preceding day. But the concept of a botanical monograph on Cyclamen was associatively connected with a number of wish-relevant thoughts, such as Freud's work on cocaine, and so the complex of associations around cocaine became operative in the dream.) The whole structure of intentional contents (the wish and related intentions, and also intentional contents that attempt to disguise the wish's object specifications, i.e. defensive intentions) co-operatively generate the life-world of dreams. So the bizarreness of the dream reflects the relatively unbridled power of unconscious intentional specifications in the absence of sensory input.

The symbolic meaning of the dream can be similarly explained. When we find a dream "symbolically meaningful," it is because we have interpreted the dream according to Freudian hermeneutics; we have translated the dreaming-life world into the unconscious wishful dream thoughts that generated it (whether by composition or *de novo* is irrelevant here). Of course, the wake life is equally symbolically meaningful. It is part of the business of the psychoanalyst to translate the wake life into unconscious wishful thoughts. The only difference between the symbolic meaningfulness with respect to unconscious wishes of the dream life and the wake life is that the former is far easier to see, since in the absence of sensory modulation the unconscious wishes dominate.

2.7 PHENOMENOLOGICAL REFLECTION AND DREAMING

We have seen that when we limit reflection to the dream life as un-reflectively lived, it is indiscernable from the wake life as unreflectively lived. We have also seen that on unlimited "studied" reflection, certain differences between dreaming and waking lives can be discerned, and that these differences are a function of the sensory disconnectedness of the sleeping condition. We now turn to a somewhat confusing because involuted topic, the discernability of dreaming and waking with respect to phenomenological reflection.

I have thus far used the term 'reflection' in a rather loose fashion, and now want to tie down what I mean by 'phenomenological reflection'. At the unreflected level of our just plain old intentional Being, our stumbling intentional existing along our world line, our practical living as human beings, we are thrown into a life-world, modally directed towards_____, where the mode might be seeing, touching, thinking, believing, desiring, etc. and the blank might be filled by any world furnishing (cabbage, king, cloud chamber track), thought, belief, feeling or whatever. In Husserl's terms, the mode is "noetic" and the blank is the object of the intentional act. Furthermore, Husserl especially emphasizes that the mode brings with it an abstract specification—the "noematic Sinn," Heidegger's "horizon," Searle's "intentional content"—which may or may not be fulfilled by an object. The noematic Sinn includes both an X component that specifies an object, and the predicate sense which specifies the object as _____, e.g. specifies a horse looking peppery gray.

Now, *reflecting is a mode too*, an abstract mode, that steps back from the world encounter so that we are directed towards the encountering rather than the world encountered. At the reflected level, the blank is filled by "horizonally and modally conscious of _____." For example, where at the unreflected level the object of my perceiving is the river, at the reflected level, the object of my reflection is an always-already-situated-I-perceiving-the-river. Heidegger points out that there is a unique being (entity) than can reflect in this way, a being for whom its own Being (to be) is at issue. Heidegger reserved "existing" for the Being (to be) of the being (entity) who might care about its Being. Put in barest terms, at the unreflected level there is an act intentionally directed on an object; at the reflected level that uniquely characterizes human existing, there is an act intentionally directed on an act/object.

Given this view of phenomenological reflection, the key question arise: What is the horizon for the reflective act? An adequate answer to this question would take us far afield from present concerns. All we need to see at present is that the philosophical horizon within which phenomenological reflection takes place is not operative while dreaming. This is at heart what Sartre and Malcolm are getting at when they insist that reflection is incompatible with the condition of dreaming.

It should *not* be thought that phenomenological reflection as defined is going on in lucid dreaming, since the horizon for such reflection does not obtain. The thought that I am dreaming takes place within whatever the dream horizon happens to be; the lucid dreamer's situatedness changes from dream to dream. The lucid dreamer does whatever he or she decides to do, and wherever he or she decides to do it, *within that dream horizon,* and that horizon is clearly not the horizon for phenomenological reflection.

The limitation of the lucid dreamer to the dream horizon given is especially emphasized by "don Juan,"[22] who relates projection of the horizon to the "assemblage point." Don Juan says that there is a "natural shift"[23] of the assemblage point that takes place during sleep, and so the horizon shifts naturally while dreaming. What the lucid dreamer does in *dreaming,* as don Juan says, is to hold on to the dream horizon after the assemblage point has shifted.

> . . . to control that shift does not mean in any way to direct it, but to keep the assemblage point fixed at the position where it naturally moves in sleep, a most difficult maneuver . . . (Castaneda 1984, p. 176)

What lucid dreamers direct is the fixation of their assemblage points.

> Seers [dreamers] are like fishermen equipped with a line that casts itself wherever it may; the only thing they can do is keep the line anchored at the place where it sinks. (Castaneda, 1984, p. 177, brackets added)

So the lucid dreamer does not sustain the horizon for phenomenological reflection, but is "at the mercy" of whatever the dream horizon happens to be and in terms of which the dreamer operates lucidly. Husserl and Heidegger seated by the fire might wonder if perhaps they are dreaming, but if they are doing phenomenology, systematically reflecting that they-are-perceiving-the-fire, then they are not dreaming.

There is no necessary reason, I think, that phenomenological reflection does not occur while dreaming; it is contingent fact. (Even if some phenomenologist-lucid dreamer might accomplish some fragmentary phenomological reflection while dreaming, it would not be sustained and systematically elaborated over many dreams. Although poets might dream the images of their poetry, existential phenomenologists do not dream their writings.) This can be easily seen in the transition to falling asleep or to awakening, when there are respectively dream-like hypnogogic and hypnopompic images (and the electrophysiological tracing is similar to REM sleep). As we drift "sleepily" into hypnogogic reverie, the "observing ego" disappears. As soon as we reflect that we are imaging, we shift towards waking and the reverie is lost. Similarly, as we drift towards awakening in hypnopompic reverie, the "observing ego" appears and the reverie evaporates. Presumably functioning of the abstract, distinctively human, brain system that supports phenomological reflection is turned on in some way by sensory input. Not only are the differences between dreaming and waking that studied reflection discerns due to the restricted sensory conditions of sleep, but the differing capacities for phenomenological reflection itself are due to those sensory conditions.

2.8 SUMMARY

I have argued for the received view, and against Sartre, Malcolm and Dennett, that we perceive a life-world while dreaming and live a life in it. We are "thrown" just as in waking. Dreaming and waking lifeworlds are indiscernable as unreflectively lived. Waking studied reflection under the dream *epoche* distinguishes dreaming to be singleminded, isolated, bizarre, symbolic, and incapable of sustained phenomenological reflection, compared to waking. These differences are accounted for by the disconnection from sensory input during sleep. During waking, sensory input serves a modulating function on operative concepts and supports the possibility of a horizon for reflection. Concepts operative during dreaming that provide the dream horizon are not modulated by input and accordingly are unbridled, persisting, and unreflective. So dreaming and waking horizons differ with respect to sensory modulation as a function of sensory restriction during sleep. This difference permits studied waking reflection to discern dreaming and waking lives, but as unreflectively lived, these lives are indiscernable.

Chapter Three

Dreaming
and Waking

> Yet the true nature of what is seen in a
> dream or visualized by the imagination ex-
> ists at all times. Everything exists in a cor-
> ner of the mind. Yogàvasistha *(Wendy
> Doniger O'Flaherty, 1984, p. 211)*

> The nagual *is the unspeakable. All the
> possible feelings and beings and selves
> float in it like barges, peaceful, unaltered,
> forever. Carlos Castaneda,* Tales of Power
> *(1974, p. 265)*

3.1 INTRODUCTION

The first step in my core argument (chapter one) was that the dream world and the life we lead in it is not a second-hand production composited together by some fantastic tinkerer, by the syntactical operations of a dream *bricoleur*, but is a continuous, spontaneous, formative production in which the dreaming life-world is constituted *de novo*. The second step (chapter two) was to argue that dreaming and waking worlds, and the unreflective lives we live in those worlds, are essentially indiscernable. The third step in the present chapter is to argue that the constitution of the dreaming life-world is anaclitic upon (leans on) the mechanism that constitutes the waking life-world. Indiscernables demand the same explanation on grounds of parsimony and biological evolution. Since the dreaming mechanism partakes of the waking mechanism, and since the dreaming mechanism is formative, then the waking mechanism is formative too (not syntactical, as the computational theory of mind would have it). That's the way my core argument goes.

We shall see that this result in which the waking life-world is also created *de novo*— rather than being there autonomously, transcendent in its own right—has strong philosophical implications. To anticipate, direct realism will be relinquished in favor of a monadological realism, in which *all* life-worlds—dreaming and waking—are constituted within an autonomous monad. The present monadology is conceived to be realistic rather than idealistic, in that the motile monadic organism is immersed within an energy sea, whose laws are captured in the equations of physical science. The flowing array of energies at the monad's interface with its surround, such as the retinal interface, come under the laws of Gibsonian "ecological optics."[1] The monad (*pace* Leibniz) has no windows through which copies of the surround might pass; nevertheless the monad is not impervious to energetic "stimuli" (literally, goads) impinging upon it. It sets up abstract specifications—the meaning component of the intentional act—and certain specifications are contingently matched by invariant abstract properties of the flowing array of energies impinging upon the monad's receptors. Those abstract specifications matched attain a special status: they are used in generating their own fulfillments within the monad in the form of the waking life-world. We are, as the sorcerer says, "enclosed within a bubble of perception." Being-in-the-world is a purely monadic affair.

The initial business of this chapter, however, is to back up to the first step of my core argument. We are sliding down a slippery slope to a monadic human condition so uncommonsensical—so "far out"—that we best check the basis of the argument. This issue is not so much with the second step—assertion of the indiscernability of unreflective dreaming and waking life-worlds—since this is just plain common opinion and philosophical tradition. (Recall Descartes doubtfully seated by the fire, wondering if he might actually be dreaming.) This second step is relatively secure, despite the criticism by Sartre, Malcolm and Dennett discussed in 2.2. I submit that Malcolm and Dennett are not really primarily concerned with dreams; they have other fish to fry. They are applying larger philosophical principles, Wittgensteinian and functionalistic respectively, to the case of dreams. That is, I think Malcolm and Dennett are into dreams "looking for trouble" because of their wider philosophical commitments—and philosophers looking for trouble are sure to find it, given the way the philosophy game is played. So if we are to check our slide down the slippery slope to a windowless monadology, then we best look to the first step, and reconsider that argument through a fresh illustration.

The argument of the first step—that the dream world and the life we lead in it is a first-hand, not a second-hand, production—does go against the mainstream, at least the western mainstream. (The mystics would not be perturbed at all by it.)[2] From Aristotle[3] to Freud to contemporary dream biology, there is unanimity that the dream life is a second-hand production, deriving from mnemic copies of the wake life. I am saying instead that the dream life is a *de novo* creation that fulfills a set of co-operative intentional acts which had previously been operative at different times during waking. The dream intentions generate their own fulfillment, like Zeus thinks Athena. Let's look again at this account of dream-life production.

3.2 The Dream of the Ocean Grotto

> *I am swimming out of the ocean into a rocky grotto. I gaze up, and against the dark vaulted ceiling I perceive a starry display of luxuriant, green, luminous growth, which I experience with a feeling of pleasurable awe.*

In reflecting on this dream, I can remember no moment of doubt that I was anything other than myself, although a certain feature of my usual self was somewhat exaggerated, in that I was highly preoccupied. I was single-mindedly caught up in what I was doing—in swimming, perceiving and feeling. I was totally absorbed, and accordingly unreflective, quite unlike the present moment of studied reflection. Dreaming is thoroughly "inauthentic" in Heidegger's sense (not "inauthentic" as an experience); the dreaming Dasein is typically quite "fallen" into the dream world, distant from its own Being. But I am often similarly singlemindedly caught up in ordinary waking life, so my lack of reflection in the dream is not exceptional. I have, then, no doubt on experiential grounds that in the dream it was really me. Even if I were to fly like a bird in my dreams, it would still feel like "me" doing the flying, like "my" world I was seeing (from a bird's-eye view).

Not only does this dream self feel like my usual self, but the dream world also seems entirely authentic. The rocky dream grotto appears just as real as if I were "actually" swimming in such a grotto, even though I have never previously gone swimming in a grotto in my life. Thus, my dream experience is both authentic and novel.

Now, the issue to be addressed is: Where did this ocean grotto and my dream life of swimming, gazing, and feeling come from? Are there mnemic copies of my wake life that might have been composited into my dream life? If not, then my dream life is freely created. I address this issue by turning to my free associations to the dream.

My immediate and compelling association to the dream is to the preceding day when I had been ruefully gazing out over my swimming pool. I had just spent a great deal of money to put a fence around the swimming pool for a specific purpose, and to mitigate my distress, I had been trying to think of some other use to which this expensive fence might be put, so that I might more favorably gloss the situation. In this vein, I had imagined (*nonvisually*) the fence supporting a plexiglass half-dome built over half the swimming pool as a windbreak and solar collector. The dream grotto with an opening to the sea had a similar shape to the plexiglass half-dome imagined over the pool during waking life.

There is another, more distant memory which I next associate to my dream experience. While driving down a wilderness road in a particularly barren area, I once unexpectedly came upon a place where water very slowly seeped into a small niche in the face of a rocky cliff. The seep looked like a miniature rock cave. It was filled with a fantastic and beautiful luminous display of green slimy growth of all kinds, an elemental, primordial life flourishing in this tiny niche of a wasteland. I had found the seep awesome and numinous. The rocky grotto of my dream had a somewhat similar but greatly magnified shape compared to the rocky seep. Also, the growth on the grotto's ceiling resembled the contents of the seep in being luminous green.

But despite the similarity of these particular memories to the dream experience, the dream grotto is not a combination or average of the (imagined) plexiglass half-dome over my pool and the rocky seep. The dream grotto is not a smoothed over shuffling together of things I had seen or imagined before. Such a synthetic operation would require a virtuoso homunculus to accomplish. (Think of taking a snapshot of a plexiglass half-dome over a swimming pool and a snapshot of a tiny seep in the face of a cliff, and trying to composit them into an ocean grotto.) The similarity between grotto, dome and seep is instead that of a family resemblance; they have a similar "look." That is, there are higher-order relational features in common across grotto, dome and seep; at an abstract level, they share the invariant structure of the half-spherical structures open at one end (just as the faces of Smith family members comprise a set of morphisms sharing an invariant structure, the typical "look" of Smith faces). Grotto, dome and seep instantiate an essential universal structure—an *eidos*—that is abstract.

Freud's conception of "family resemblance" is that the dream object concatenates properties of previously experienced objects or averages across them. But the grotto of my dream is not a patchwork assemblage or collage of the dome and seep, or a blurry average of the dome and seep. (Recall that I did not even see the dome, *but had only imagined it.* The dome of my wake life was entirely abstract, an unfulfilled signitive act.) Instead, the abstract invariant structure across grotto, dome and seep implies a common prototype that they all instantiate, abstract specifications that they all meet. During waking, my imaginative act directed on the dome and my perceptual act directed on the seep were directed via certain partially common abstract specifications. During dreaming, my intentions generate the dream experience via those common abstract specifications. Thus, the past provides not mnemic copies of waking perceptual images to be used for populating dreams, but abstract meanings for generating the dream.

Let us turn to the unconscious wishes that are fulfilled by the dream according to Freud's theory. Although I call these wishes "unconscious," they are not totally foreign to me. It is just that I am not fully "in touch" with them, and am ordinarily unaware of how greatly these wishes affect my waking life. They are more in the nature of "unfinished business," where the "business" cuts to the existential core of Dasein.

The swimming pool has been an expensive and untrustworthy companion of mine for many years. (I have often referred to it as my "worthy adversary!") An ugly growth of algae is favored by its walls. I don't even really like to swim, and if it weren't for its virtually inaccessible location, I would have filled it in a long time ago. The occasion for building the fence is that the twins anticipated in the dream of chapter one are now toddlers, and my wife and I are anxious to protect them from falling into the clutches of my nemesis.

The birth of the twins, moreover, has affected my life in other ways. I had previously spent many years with great personal freedom. Before the twins, I had traveled and had some awesome experiences of nature, such as finding the luxuriant seep in a wasteland; I had felt that I was living life fully. Now, I have to stay at home (by the swimming pool). No more viewing a spectacular starry sky in the California mountains! (At home, by the swimming pool, there is too much haze to appreciate the night sky.)

My dream seems to fulfill certain wishes that have been greatly activated by my immediate life situation since the arrival of the twins. My persecutor, the ugly swimming pool, is replaced by a beautiful grotto in which I happily swim and behold sights more marvelous even than when I could travel. My deep wish to experience life fully is gratified as I perceive this green luminosity.

However, the birth of the twins has not just been a negative occasion, a constraint on my freedom to live, but also a positive opportunity to refresh my spirit though contact with their elemental life force. In the dream I am in pleasurable awe of a primordial symbol of life, the luxuriant green growth. Indeed, the symbolism of ocean, grotto and primordial life suggest that at a deeper level, there is a wish for rebirth gratified in the dream. Thus, this is a very satisfying dream at both material and spiritual levels.

Let us now consider how these wishes provide specifications for generating the dream. As I initially emphasized, from the standpoint of our own reflection we are ourselves in dreams. A sometimes fantastic and sometimes ordinary world is present to us, and we take actions in it. We are, however, exceptionally preoccupied in the dream with our own actions and the world that we take these actions in. In the enraptured pursuit of dream chimeras we unreflectively act out our wishes.

In terms of the present dream, I am given in my dream a world of ocean and rocky grotto. This world is given via two specifications: first, the invariant structure of dome and seep which accounts for their family resemblance, and second, specifications not shared across dome and seep, but associated with one or the other. An example of the second case is that the imagining of the plexiglass dome over half the pool necessarily included the open half of the pool. There is a family resemblance between (imagining) swimming from the open half of the pool to under the plexiglass dome on the one hand, and swimming from the open ocean into the grotto. But there is no family resemblance in this regard between the seep and the grotto; the seep was so miniature that I could never enter it, and it did not even have pooled water. Again, there is a family resemblance between the rockiness of the seep and the grotto, while the pool is smooth plaster.

Given a world so specified, what am I doing in it? For one thing, I am being very adventurous, confidently swimming around in an ocean grotto. (In waking life, I would have been worried about sharks!) I am making the most of my freedom . . . living fully the world available to me . . . experiencing awe at primordial life . . . and feeling refreshed. Thus I attentively act in my dream in accordance with the plans that guide the attainment of my wishes.

It is apparent that the dream world and the dreamer's actions in it are coherent, since the same specifications generate both. I long for adventure, I generate the adventurous setting of ocean and grotto, and I act adventurously in it. I long for contact with the life force, I generate the display of primordial green growth, and I feel awe towards it. Thus, the dream world and my "natural" actions in it are easily coupled.

It should not be thought that the hegemony of the wish extends only to our dream actions; the wish also holds sway over invariants from the past. To illustrate, note that the dome is a day residue of emotional significance and that in my life prior to the day of the dream there have been a whole family of things I have seen bearing a resemblance to the dome. Why should the seep in particular be involved in the dream? It is only because the seep represents for me a time of freedom when currently active wishes were actually satisfied. Presumably other members of the family do not have this significance. From the family of memories resembling the dome, that individual memory marked by wish-gratification is chosen. But the dream wish does not elicit a mnemic copy of the seep; it activates invariant specifications that characterize the seep, and these specifications are joined with other specifications in generating an authentic and novel dream world in which I act so as to gratify my wishes.

So discussion of my dream of the ocean grotto comes to the same place as the dreams discussed in chapter one. The dream is not secondhand from copies of the wake life. It is "somehow" freely created, and the act of creation derives from certain waking intentional acts re-operative while dreaming.

I want to emphasize that the rejection of Freud's theory is ultimately to be based not on *my* dreams, but on *your* dreams. That is, my reflections on my dreams are to be understood as an invitation to you to coreflect on your own dreams, and to see if they are second-hand or at least to some extent authentic creations. Could your dream scene and your correlated actions in it have been stitched together from your past waking scenes and actions? Or does it have only a family resemblance to your waking experiences, a novel presentation of family classes encountered and actions taken during your waking? I think dream phenomenology has been mainly unexplored (save for Rechtschaffen and Foulkes),[4] and my claims in this regard are properly construed as invitations to coreflect on dream appearances.

3.3 From Dream Life to Wake Life

We saw in the last chapter that the unreflective dream life is essentially indiscernable from the unreflective wake life, and that the differences apparent to waking reflection can be accounted for by the difference between the sleeping and waking condition with regard to the functional absence or presence of sensory input to brain mechanisms. Only the most compelling of reasons should prevent the conclusion that the mechanism underlying the dream life is fundamentally the same as the mechanism underlying the wake life. Indiscernables demand the same explanation. If the dreaming life-world is constituted formatively, then so must the waking life-world. Any other conclusion would make a mockery of the law of parsimony.

The powerful reluctance to draw this conclusion mainly derives, I believe, from the existential consequences: the scary monadic condition of human beings wherein each of us is enclosed within a "bubble of perception," the existential isolation of beings who realize that other humans are but "apparitions" constituted within the monadic bubble, the poignant uniqueness and responsibility of each of us on our own version of a lonely "journey to Ixtlan."[5] Even the movers and shakers of existentialism—Heidegger, Sartre, Merleau-Ponty (and their progenitor, Husserl)—could mitigate the loneliness of the human condition in virtue of their (however inconsistently held) direct realism; at least we are in direct (ek-static) contact with a real world.[6] But if the present argument goes through, then our homey world and all our warm fellow creatures in it disappear as we usually think of them. We live out the drama and dullness of our lives, our anguish, joy and indifference, our loves and hates, each for our self alone. This makes the present conclusion difficult to accept. (For the mystic, acceptance of the true state of the human condition—acceptance of *māyā*—supports the numinous turn from life-world to Spirit.)

There is in addition to parsimony a bioevolutionary argument that constrains us to demand the same explanation for dreaming and waking life-worlds. A bioevolutionary argument is tainted for mainstream philosophy, which holds that philosophy is foundational to science and that ever-changing science is not a firm basis for ontology. Nevertheless, I think that philosophical conclusions ought at least to *fit* evolutionary science, which is highly advanced and most unlikely to change in ways relevant to the present argument. If your theory, no matter how plausible, doesn't plausibly cohere with biology, then you would be well advised to let go of it. I think that is the case here, for the following reasons.

Suppose we ask: How would a brain mechanism have developed in evolution with the capacity for generating life-worlds *de novo* while dreaming? (A philosopher who would want to deny that the dream life supervenes on brain mechanisms has no basis for discussion with the present writer. Here I would agree with Wittgenstein and Malcolm that philosophers need to know when to stop asking questions!) The life-world as dreamed has no value for survival or procreation as such, so why should such an amazing capacity be selected in evolution? That I am capable of dream-thinking up an ocean grotto does not help to pass on my genes. It is quite obviously perception of the waking life-world that has selective advantage. Perception of the dreaming life-world would be anaclitic upon waking mechanisms, according to sensible evolutionary concepts, with one possible exception, I think.

The exception might be argued that the dream life is just a mere *byproduct* of some important biological process going on during sleep; that is, the dream life is neurophysiologically epiphenomenal, without function or consequence. This idea is prima facie implausible, in that it holds that a mere byproduct of some basic activity can be indiscernable from one of the very highest of evolutionary achievements. We have already seen and rejected one such theory by Hobson and McCarley in which, in effect, the brain stem mechanically starts sending up random or quasi-random signals, during the periodic activation of REM sleep; these signals are mechanically best fitted to memory traces; and the REM-sleepy forebrain is then mechanically forced to synthesize the memory traces thus selected into the dream-life, "making the best of a bad job." Similarly for Crick and Mitchison, the dream is a mere byproduct of the serious business of reaming out memory stores of "unwanted parasitic modes." Again, for Greenberg, during sleep there is a transfer of information from short term to long-term memory, and the dream-life is just an incidental byproduct of this information transfer.

Evans makes the following proposal along these lines.

> ... suppose that the short-term [memory] system could hold information circulating, so to speak, in an immediate-access store, but that the system was unable to keep this information indefinitely "on hold." At night, with sensory input reduced, some part of the brain would now get to work on the data pool, sorting out the material into "wanted" and "unwanted," filing the data according to whether it would be needed for immediate-access or long-term store. The REM periods with their accompanying phases of hyper-activity might represent the sorting and transferring process. (Evans, 1984, p. 140, bracket added)

In the dream, then, there is "a momentary interception by the conscious mind of material being sorted, scanned, sifted or whatever."[7] When this happens our conscious mind gets "a glimpse of the programs being run

[and] an attempt is made by the conscious brain to 'interpret' it as a kind of pseudo-event and a dream is remembered."[8] Again, as in Hobson and McCarley, what is basically happening is that the REM-sleepy brain synthesizes the mass of memory traces being sorted through into an intelligible life-world. So according to these proposals, the computer brain during REM sleep is accomplishing some essential mechanical function, and the dream life is a peculiar byproduct of this basic process.

But no proposal will do that makes the dream life a byproduct of some other process that makes use of mnemic copies of the wake life, since we have seen that there is no responsible way of getting from such memories to the dream life without invoking a dream homunculus to effect the synthesis. Is there some other mechanism of creativity, then, that dream creativity might lean on?

The mechanism for imagination is one that we might naturally think of as perceptually formative. Waking imagination, however, seems pale compared to the dream. Indeed, writers from Sartre to Pylyshn[9] in the contemporary mainstream deny that in imagination there is any image, any faint copy, of some sensible object. Sartre says,

> . . . the *flesh* of the object is not the same in an image and in a perception. By "flesh" I understand the intimate texture. The classical authors describe the image as a faint, vague perception but in all other respects like the perception in the "flesh." Now we know this to be in error. (Sartre, 1940, p. 21)

For Sartre, imagination is an empty intentional state whose contents "envision" (i.e. specify) sensible properties of perceivable objects.

> This imaginative consciousness may be said to represent in the sense that it goes out in search of its object in the realm of perception and that it envisions [specifies] the sensible elements that constitute this realm. . . . it is spontaneous and creative; it maintains and sustains the sensible qualities of its object by a continuous creation. (Sartre, 1940, p. 20, bracket added)

After all, when I imagined the plexiglass half-dome over the swimming pool I did not actually *see* any such dome in my "mind's eye," in the way that I saw the grotto of my dream; I just *conceived* it. If waking imagination is not formatively creative, as Sartre and Pylyshn think, then dreaming creativity cannot lean on its mechanism.

But suppose we go against the mainstream position on imagination, with Kosslyn and Foulkes, and say that the imaginary intentional act is not empty but filled with a concrete image. The image is admittedly paler in imagination but that is because of competition by sensory input. When input is blocked in the sleep state, the mechanism of imagination operates unimpeded in its full glory.

So waking imagination and dreaming share a common formatively creative mechanism according to this view. The capacity to form waking images, however pale, has survival advantage and is selected, and the vivid dream images show this capacity in its fullest expression. Dreaming is just an especially vivid imagining, and is anaclitic upon the mechanism of waking imagining, not waking perception.

This view assimilating dreaming to waking imagination is implausible, however, since the dream life is indiscernable from the ordinary wake life and discernable from the life imagined during waking. Even if I take my most vivid waking imagination, which is in sexual fantasy, it is easily discernable from the waking sexual life; it is "as if" there were a sexual partner, whereas a sexual dream seems like the full-on thing. If dreaming is to be assimilated to something else, this is properly to its indiscernable, not to its discernable. Indeed, to be parsimonious and consistent with evolution, the more likely possibility is that the "pale" imagined life is anaclitic upon the mechanism that generates indiscernable wake and dream lives; so *if* the imagined world is concretely present, *contra* the mainstream, this is to be taken as an instance of formative creativity in the act of imagining.

There is another possibility of waking formative creativity, which Foulkes[10] brings out, that dreaming formative creativity might be anaclitic upon. There do seem to be *fragmentary* dreams during waking, but these occur only *under special conditions* when a person is relaxed, with eyes shut, and relinquishes voluntary control of mental processes. Even if someone might constitute an authentic life-world under such conditions, what would be its evolutionary value? Why should evolution bifurcate at its very pinnacle into two different but equi-productive mechanisms, a waking mechanism with powerful survival and reproductive value and a waking-dream mechanism without obvious value? Again, there must be one basic mechanism, that of waking, to which the waking-dream is assimilated.

Are there any other candidates for waking formative creativity? Certainly not illusion; this is just misperception of what is given. Hallucination, perhaps. The mechanism of hallucination might well overlap with that of dreaming creativity. But surely hallucination is not selected in evolution. Since I can't think of any other possibilities (and given my critique of all mnemic copy theories), the formative mechanism for constituting the dreaming life-world must lean upon the mechanism for constituting the waking life-world, and the latter mechanism must be formative, too.

3.4 THE LIFE-WORLD AS MODEL

Having raised the evolutionary issues of adaptation, survival and reproduction in 3.3, the question arises: If the life-world of waking is formatively created, what insures that it adequately models the surrounding so that the monadic organism might fit its niche? What in the present theory assures that the life-world constituted during waking well models the source of input?

For the traditional causal theory of perception, the correspondence between model and surrounding is no problem. Since input order is *conserved* across a sequence of neural transformations, this assures that the life-world perceived models the real world (in its *structural* properties). The conserved information is a kind of copy that ties the life-world to an inferred reality. The traditional view, at heart, conceives of sensory input as a message from the external reality. (In Descartes for example, the message is carried to the pineal gland where it is communicated to mind.) This message is variously subject to analysis, comparison, transformation, abstraction, classification, interpretation, and so on, such that by the time the message appears in consciousness, as a phenomenal object, it is enormously enriched, but still conserves the original message. So it is the brute conservation of input order that warrants the model of reality.

The present theory in contrast conceives of sensory input as regulative of mechanisms for constituting the perceived world. There is no message received from the external reality and copied. Instead a model of reality is created (generated, constituted) *de novo* according to abstract specifications afforded by input. So there is no order conserved, no representations processed, in the present theory (and no "hyletic data" [Husserl]). Yet the order of reality must be somehow conserved in the experienced life-world constituted by abstract entities. After all, the model must work. The question still remains: What fits the contents of the monadic "bubble of perception" to its surrounding?

To answer this question we must turn to the life-world as it appears to us, in order to appreciate just what kind of model it is. Now things we perceive have a "look" to them. ("Look" or "appearance" is the original meaning of *eidos*.)[11] This thing looks like a tree, that thing looks like a house, and that "ambiguous figure" looks like a duck and then like a rabbit (the input affording two distinct classifications). We "take" things to be what they look like.

Now, any "look" requires a bearer. There is no look of a Cheshire grin without the cat to bear it. Without the cat's fulfilling function, the Cheshire grin can be only an empty abstract entity, an *eidos* in the sense developed by Plato, a thought which has no look to it at all. How, then, is the bearer constituted?[12]

But this bearer also has a look. A distant red barn in Mendocino has the look of something with sides and a back, and it also has the look of Mendocino red. We never are conscious of any primordial meaningless red sensation which is "red as such." Perceived red is always "taken" in some way—has a certain look—say, the look of a red color patch rather than the look of a red barn.

Certain of the looks we perceive, then, are looks of bearers, more traditionally termed "phenomenal qualities" such as color and brightness, pitch and loudness, softness, sour and acrid. There are also qualities of feeling and wanting, visceral, kinesthetic and temporal qualities, and even thetic qualities that might be held to bear thoughts.[13] What distinguishes the look of bearers is that it is an *irreducible* (or first-order) look. To borrow Sellars' example, the look of a ladder can be analyzed into the look of "being cylindrical (the rungs), rectangular (the frame), wooden, etc."[14], but the pink look of a homogeneously pink ice cube can't be further analyzed; it looks "pink through and through."

These first-order looks which cannot be further analyzed are a function of input order in that electromagnetic input in a certain range of frequencies matches the intentional specification of "red," and in virtue of the match enables the intention to constitute the look of red. In effect, the input signal enables certain rules to become operative in constituting looks of the world. For another example, certain abstract properties of the flowing array of energies impinging upon my eyes as I drive down a country road—having to do with retinal disparity between the eyes, texture gradients, relative motion, etc—match the specification "distant," which is enabled to constitute the distant look of a red barn in Mendocino.

This theory of perception functionally entails input selecting rules for constituting looks, rather than input being conserved as sense data, hyletic data, sensa, or whatever the representation. (This is reminiscent of the adverbial theory of perception, in which we do not perceive a red sensation but "sense redly;" that is, "redly" *qua* rule of sensing constitutes the first-order look of red. Of course, the adverbial theory, unlike the present theory, is directly realistic.) So intentions whose abstract conditions have been satisfied (in Husserl's terms, noetic acts under noematic prescriptions that have been fulfilled) generate looks, some of which are irreducible looks of bearers.

We are now in a position to return to the question of how the monadic bubble of perception fits its surrounding. *If* the abstract specifications generated within the monad comprise a good theory of the surrounding, then input will be properly matched. It will follow that the life-world constituted by the matched specifications will adequately model the source of input. The model is warranted not by the conservation of input order but by the appropriateness of those abstract specifications that the input flux matches. That is, input affords certain specifications, and these specifications are enabled to constitute a certain "look" of an object. Abstract specifications thus map onto looks. If the theory of the surrounding (both innate and learned) is a good one, then the input will be well modeled. *Thus input (and its source) maps onto abstract specifications which map onto looks of the world.* If the organism holds meanings that comprise an appropriate theory of its environmental sources of input, it will be able to constitute a life-world that models the reality in a good enough fashion that survival and reproduction are assured. (I follow W. Weimer[15] here, who argues in a Platonic vein that the organism is a theory of its environment.) The actual mechanism by which the life-world is constituted will be considered in the next chapter.

3.5 Philosophical Commitments

The present commitment is to monadological *realism*, not idealism. This realistic framework is only partially shared with Leibniz. Leibniz scholars, in any case, do not agree on how to interpret Leibniz's monadology.[16] The basic idea of monadological realism as developed here is that each of us is a monad, a system (autonomous entity, a being), with an inherent creative principle. The creative principle of the monad continuously produces a life-world *de novo*, constitutes a "bubble of perception."[17] The monad moving within its niche is surrounded by a reality (also containing other monads), is immersed in an energy sea that physical science captures in its mathematical equations.

Pace Leibniz, there are no "windows" in the monad through which copies of reality might get in. (Nor are there, as Heidegger requires, any fenestrations out of which *ekstases* are always already passed to the world.) At the interface between monad and surrounding reality are not windows but matched filters. The filters in effect ring to abstract invariant properties within the input flux; they match higher-order invariant relations within the input flux. The filters matched shape the monad's inherent creative perceptual process, in a way described in the next chapter. Accordingly, the perceptual world produced veridically reflects the stable (invariant) source of the energy flux at the filters.

One other feature of the present monadological realism deserves mention. The monad's filters are not just fixed, hard-wired, passive devices. The filters are *continuously tuned* by higher mechanisms internal to the monad. (All or many of the filters are "cognitively penetrable.")[18] The monad's "pick up" of invariant properties within the input flux is in effect a *matching process*. The tuning of filters sets up abstract specifications (Husserl's noematic prescriptions) which the abstract properties of the input flux variously meet. The tuning process can be thought of along Searlean lines as *intentional,* with the tuning specifications as the intentional content which sets up conditions of satisfaction. (Searle is an archetypal direct realist, and would have none of the present monadological realism.) Rather than talking (in a Neisserian vein) of a tuned filter "picking up" invariant information from reality, we might better talk of invariant information from reality "picking out" (selecting) tunings in virtue of satisfying those tunings. The tunings thus picked out inform generation of the perceptual world.

The present philosophical commitments only make sense if dreaming is taken seriously, more formally, taken under the double phenomenological epoche. Such a monadological conception is extremely counter-intuitive, and can be quite annoying to direct realists who think with common sense that they immediately encounter the real world rather than hoisting it within an autonomous bubble of perception. To lose the world that anchors our existing is yet another narcissistic blow, as in the Copernican, Darwinian and Freudian revolutions, which respectively decentered man's place of abode, his nature, and his conscious knowing. Better write off dreaming as "chimerical"—literally, a mythic fire-spouting female monster—then lose our cozy world!

The present monadological realism sounds so similar to a common idea in transpersonal psychology, that I want again to distinguish it. This common idea is that we "create" an illusory world in virtue of our interpretations, i.e. the ego *distorts* "true reality." Thus, the following quotes taken from *A course in miracles* superficially seem to say the same thing as monadological realism.[19]

Dreams show you that you have the power to make a world as you would have it be, and that because you want it you see it.

> And while you see it you do not doubt that it is real. Yet here is
> a world, clearly within your mind, that seems to be outside.[20]

For this view, effect and cause are interchanged, such that the maker of
the dream believes that what he made is happening to him. This all
sounds like formative creativity.

But there is a commitment to the compositional theory of dream
world formation: The dreamer does not realize he "picked a thread from
here, a scrap from there, and wove a picture out of nothing."[21] The idea
here is that we *distort* the true world by our own wishes. "Dreams are
perceptual temper tantrums, in which you literally scream, 'I want it
thus!' And thus it seems to be."[22] The wake world is also distorted.

> You seem to waken, and the dream is gone. Yet what you fail to
> recognize is that what caused the dream has not gone with it.
> Your wish to make another world that is not real remains with
> you. And what you seem to waken to is but another form of this
> same world you see in dreams. All your time is spent in dream-
> ing. Your sleeping and your waking dreams have different forms,
> and that is all. Their content is the same. They are your protest
> against reality, and your fixed and insane idea that you can
> change it.[23]

Both waking and dreaming the ego is unable to tolerate reality as it is and
wants to change it to suit itself, substituting illusion for truth. But the present monadological view of waking does not simply hold that we distort
what is truly world, truly real. *Even the world perceived undistortedly,
without ego, the world seen in Truth by those enlightened, remains formatively created.*

3.6 Summary

The mechanism that underlies formation of the dreaming life-world
is anaclitic upon a waking mechanism, on grounds of both parsimony

and evolution. In waking, sensory input influences the world generated by picking out certain tunings of filters on input. The tunings thus picked out determine formative generation of the life-world. In dreaming, certain tunings from waking become reoperative and determine the life-world of dreams. In each case, dreaming and waking, the monadic organism generates a life-world *de novo* by abstract means.

Chapter Four

The Cognitive Approach To Dreaming

. . . dreaming must be seen as something more than anomalous perceiving. It is a human conceptual achievement of the first magnitude, and one of the core problems of cognitive psychology. Dreaming needs once again, as it was by Freud, to be recognized as a problem so central to the study of the mind that its resolution can help to reveal the fundamental structures of human thought.
David Foulkes, A Grammar of Dreams.
(1978, p. 6)

4.1 INTRODUCTION

We have seen that dreaming and waking are equally formatively creative. A life-world is continuously generated *de novo* in both. So perilous the human condition! Enclosed within a bubble of perception, we create worlds and our lives in them both dreaming and waking. Lost in *māyā*, we say commonsensically that the waking life-world is real and the dreaming life-world chimerical, but they are equivalently our productions.

We are windowless monads. We set up abstract specifications, and detect matchings with abstract properties of the flowing array of energies at our receptive interfaces with the surrounding reality. We monads think abstract conditions and register their satisfaction. This monadic opening to reality does not permit copies, but only detects that certain monadic specifications have been fulfilled. The specifications matched then generate the life-world *de novo*. But how? By what mechanism might we think up concrete worlds and our lives in them, just like that? *What kind of a machine could be formatively creative?*

A computer isn't. A computer is syntactically creative, like a bricoleur combining found elements into a new arrangement. Formative creativity doesn't seem to fit with what we think of as machine capabilities. If we could only point to *some* machine that is formatively creative, then this would suggest that if we looked around a bit, maybe we would find other formatively creative machines. Maybe even the brain is a wet one, and so *our* formative creativity could supervene upon it. I attempt to show in this chapter that the immune system is in fact formatively creative, and then consider the brain in that regard, looking over to optical information processing system technology.

My claim that a computer can't generate the dream world and our life in it will of course not go unchallenged. Foulkes argues forcefully in his *Dreaming: A Cognitive-Psychological Analysis* (1985) that a computer-like brain can and does produce the dreaming life-world. So the initial business of this chapter is critiquing the cognitive approach to dreaming. I begin by discussing Neisser, who changed horses from the very influential *Cognitive Psychology* (1967) to the Gibsonian *Cognition and Reality* (1976). (Gibson here is suitably cognitivized by addition of Neisserian schemata.) I then turn to Foulkes, who quite single-handedly, I think, has thought through how dreams relate to cognitive science. In his earlier *A Grammar of Dreams* (1978), Foulkes gives a psycholinguistic version of Freud's theory. But Foulkes (1985) later pulls free of Freud, and elaborates a consistent theory of dreaming in purely cognitive terms. After the critique of the current cognitive approach to dreams, which thinks that computers can handle dreams, I finally turn to the topic of the formatively creative machine that might produce them.

4.2 THE COGNITIVE APPROACH

According to the mainstream of cognitive science—"the computational theory of mind" with its representations and processings—

the waking mind is *treated as* an abstract formalized system, or a kind of computer that transforms (rearranges) symbolic tokens. (Haugeland[1] traces this computational view back to Hobbes.) These tokens are exact, i.e. "digital," and the transformings (rearrangings) are "syntactical." The waking mind thus conceived as abstract machine admittedly supervenes on a wet machine, the human brain, but the actual neural realization is of no interest to the functionalistic cognitivist. Of course, sometimes it aids thought to think in actual machine terms, but here the cognitivist would prefer silicon to neural terms. Since we build and program computers, it is easier to think about them rather than about the brain, whose machinery far surpasses our understanding; technology thus captures our thought and turns us into "Turing's men."[2]

Extrapolating over to dreaming, the dreaming mind is also an abstract machine and computer-like in actual operation. Now, Freud's theory of dream world formation could be (mistakenly) thought to run on a computer. Let the machine tokens be mnemic copies, let the syntactical rearranging of these tokens be the process of compositing mnemic copies, toss in a fancy "smoothing subroutine" to play the role of the synthetic function—and out pops the dreaming life-world! But the cognitive approach denies mnemic copies. Remembering is *not* "a matter of opening old file drawers," Neisser says, but rather, "we store traces of earlier cognitive acts, not of the products of those acts."[3] Furthermore, striking experimental evidence from cognitive psychology which shows that the dream world is not a synthetic composition of mnemic copies has been obtained by Kerr, Foulkes and Schmidt.

Laboratory dream reports were obtained from two subjects who became legally blind as teenagers. Their dream visualizations were like their waking visual experience *before* they became blind. Of especial importance to the present discussion, it was found that the dream visual imagery of these subjects "included well defined imaginal representations of people and places known only *since* the acquisition of blindness."[4] *Such dream imagery could not have been derived from mnemic copies,* because of the subjects' blindness. So the cognitive approach to dreaming rejects Freud's compositional theory, and accordingly, is faced with the task of accounting for dreaming formative creativity by use of a purely digital and syntactical device.

4.3 Neisser's Dream Theory

Neisser (1976) has briefly discussed a theory of dream perception which I shall flesh out.[5] But first we need to understand Neisser's later theory of perception and its relation to Gibson.

4.3a Neisserian Perception

Gibson's thesis was that perception is *the direct pickup of information* from sensory input to the organism. Input is conceived very dynamically, in that the organism is immersed within an ever-changing "energy sea" and is itself in motion. So there is a "flowing array" of stimulus energies impinging on the organism's receptors; the stimulus is in continual flux. Gibson saw a fundamental problem in accounting for the perception of a stable world when the organism is given a stimulus flux. Gibson emphasized that the stimulus doesn't give little pictures of the world to the brain.

> So when I assert that perception of the environment is direct, I mean that it is not mediated by *retinal* pictures, *neural* pictures or *mental* pictures. (Gibson, 1979, p. 147)

Gibson's solution to the problem of perceptual constancy was that there are *abstract* properties within the flowing array that are *invariant*.

To illustrate, as we walk around a rectangular table there is a flowing succession of trapezoidal projections on the retina, yet the table *looks rectangular* the whole time.

> Although the changing angles and proportions of the set of trapezoidal projections are a fact, the *unchanging relations* among the four angles, and the *invariant proportions* over the set are another fact, equally important, and they uniquely specify the rectangular surface. (Gibson, 1979, p. 74, emphasis added)

Perception of a stable world, then, is just the pickup of abstract invariant information from the flowing array of energies at the sensory receptors.

Neisser adds to Gibson the importance of cognitive factors ("schemata") that ready the organism to pick up certain kinds of information. (But he does not go so far as Fodor and Pylyshn, who add Helmholtzian inference to Gibson.) Schemata anticipate abstract invariants.[6] Perception *qua* direct pickup of invariant information is for Neisser penetrated by cognition.

4.3b Neisserian Dreaming

In the case of dreaming, it is apparent that there is no stimulus informational flux so there is nothing to detect. In this regard, Neisser groups dreams with motion pictures, after-images, double images, and hallucinations. For these latter, there is

> a kind of "simulation"; that is, the perceiver is being systematically misinformed. Either the real environment or a part of his visual system is simulating an object by providing some of the information that would be available if the object were actually present. The mechanism of simulation is obvious for motion pictures, and hardly less obvious in the case of after-images, double images, and similar phenomena. (Neisser, 1976, p. 31)

Neisser has no account, however, of how the information might be simulated for cognitive processing during dreaming since he adamantly does not admit concrete memory traces that copy (more precisely, conserve) the order of the waking world.

Neisser is not concerned about this lack, however. He wants to deny that there is any such thing as perceptual images during dreaming anyway, and so he thinks he doesn't have to account for any life-world formation. He assimilates dreaming to imagining, which is for Neisser a purely empty cognitive activity, an anticipation of information. (Cf. Sartre and 2.2a)

> Perceiving, like locomotion, is a cyclic activity that includes anticipation and information pickup. Any delay between the anticipation and the pickup creates a state of unfulfilled perceptual readiness, and the inner aspect of that active schema is a mental image. To conjure up an image of a shark in a crib is simply to prepare oneself to look at one, making ready to pick up the information that such an unlikely spectacle would offer. (Neisser, 1976, p. 138)

Dreams accordingly would be purely "propositional," like Pylyshn's account of waking imagery.[7] No formative creativity is required since dreams are wholly thought-like.

But this would be so at variance with the experience of most people that one is led to argue, in *ad hominem* fashion, that some people—maybe the people who are most successfully cognitive during waking—must just happen to have only cognitive dreams. To deny that there is any perceptual world during dreaming that needs assimilating to waking perception is *prima facie* implausible. (See the detailed discussion of this point in 2.2.) And so the issue of forming the dreaming life-world cannot be avoided, as the later Neisser did.

The earlier Neisser *was* vitally concerned with how abstract cognitions might generate concrete worlds.[8] In this frame dream images are "synthesized," and therein hangs a tale. Dreaming is assimilated to imaging, and imaging is not empty (as in later Neisser) but is assimilated to perceiving.

> Believing that the processes of imagery are also those of perception, I will use the verb "see," hereafter without quotation marks, with respect to them. Believing that these processes also create the vivid visual phantasms of dreams and psychoses, I will occasionally use the term "image" in this connection as well. An image, even an unclear one, is called a "hallucination" if the subject believes that what he sees really exists; otherwise it is just an image, no matter how vivid it happens to be. (Neisser, 1967, p. 146)

Dreaming, imaging and perceiving are all synthetic constructive activities.

> ... images will be treated here as products of visual synthesis. If visual cognition is an active and constructive process in "perceiving," when there is much relevant information in the retinal image, it must continue to be so when stored information is primarily involved. Imagery is not a matter of opening old file drawers, but of building new models. (Neisser, 1967, p. 146)

Neisser clearly raises the crucial issue of the present discussion:

If images are constructions, what is their raw material? (Neisser, 1967, p. 280)

... the metaphor of construction implies some raw material. (Neisser, 1967, p. 284)

He of course denies the representational tradition of British empiricist philosophers (like Hobbes, Locke, Hume and Mill) where there are "ideas" that are "slightly faded copies of sensory experiences."[9] Imagery, including dream imagery, is based on stored information, but such memory traces are not copies of past experiences; they are traces of *prior processes of construction*. So the raw materials for dream construction, according to the earlier Neisser, are synthesizing acts, i.e. cognitive operations, derived from waking synthesizing cognitive acts reoperative during REM sleep.

But at first blush this will not do. The act of construction requires raw materials to work upon. The mason requires stone to construct a fireplace; the painter requires paints to paint a picture; even the Demiurge requires chaos to form cosmos. Accepting that there are memory traces of past synthesizing acts that are reoperative during REM sleep, the theory of construction still needs some raw material for the synthetic acts to work with. No copies (representations, sensa, hyletic data) are admitted by Neisser, so the "raw material" is mysterious indeed. It is apparent that we need to unpack just what Neisser could mean by "synthesize."

Actually, Neisser waffles considerably on the copy issue, despite his protestations. Following Hebb, he compares the perceiver to a paleontologist

who carefully extracts a few fragments of what might be bones from a mass of irrelevant rubble and "reconstructs" the dinosaur that will eventually stand in the Museum of Natural History. In this sense it is important to think of focal attention as a constructive, synthetic activity rather than as purely analytic. One does not simply examine the input and make a decision; one *builds* an appropriate visual object. (Neisser, 1967, p. 94)

Thus "all perceiving is a constructive process" guided by the abstract information picked up.[10]

But how then are we to interpret the few bone fragments of the paleontologist? If fragmentary copies are allowed—just a few old bones to build on—then we are back to all the traditional problems of mnemic copies, now copies impoverished. Indeed, a few pages later Neisser mentions the fragments of bone and goes on to comment that preattentive processes "make only chunks of raw material, out of which focal attention may sythesize many different products."[11] So one tendency in Neisser is illegitimately to slip copies *qua* primitive raw material back into the theory.[12]

But given the widespread disenchantment with copy theories across contemporary psychology, brain science and philosophy, let's consider the possibilities for synthesis sans copies. No one really wants mnemic copies, but do we need them? Is it possible to do without them in virtue of some kind of "synthesis?" The prospects for Neisser's cognitive approach to dreams depends on unpacking what "synthesis" means.

Note that it is unattractive for a cognitive science to read "synthesize" as a creation *ex nihilo*, as if perceptual information were created from scratch, for such a process is completely obscure, indeed anomalous with respect to physical law. Creation *ex nihilo* is the province not of machines, but of God, the *ens encreatum*, the uncreated Creator, who lies outside the domain of physical law.

Nor can the cognitive approach tolerate reading "synthesize" as the activities of a Platonic Demiurge (literally, "craftsman") shaping chaos into the world and its heavenly spheres, like a potter shapes the clay in accordance with the *eidos* of the pot to be produced. In the Platonic story, primacy shifts to the Demiurge's Idea, and the machine dwindles to a more technical matter like the potter's wheel.

Unfortunately, it is not at all clear just what Neisser really does mean by "synthesis." In his later book, the whole problem drops away (his great shift barely remarked by Neisser) in favor of Gibsonian pick-up. No synthesis is needed if perceptual information is there for the picking up in the input flux. Let us proceed then, to Foulkes' discussion, in the hope of finally clarifying the possibilities for synthesis.

4.4 FOULKES' APPROACH

Foulkes' (1978, 1982) earlier approach to the problem of forming the life-world of dreams is through a linguistic analogy (1.4d). He defines the discipline of "psychoneirics" as

> the cognitive-psychological study of the processes of dreaming, and it is meant to stand in relation to dream phenomena as psycholinguistics does to linguistic phenomena. (Foulkes, 1982, p. 170)

Foulkes sees abstract mechanisms generating dream images in the way that abstract mechanisms generate utterances.

> I propose that both speaking and dreaming originate with representations of knowledge that are abstracted generalizations from and interpretations and elaborations of, our perceptual experience. (Foulkes, 1982, p. 176)

> I shall assume that the sources of dream imagery lie in forms of long-term knowledge representation that are abstract, and that deal either with the meanings and functional properties of objects or events—abstract meaning memory—or with the rules by which the physical properties of objects and events can be transformed into meanings, and vice versa. (Foulkes, 1982, p. 175)

Foulkes (1985) holds to this primacy of the abstract in his most recent work. Knowledge representation in memory is not quasi-pictorial (analog) but abstract, "representing meanings in a nonpictorial, nonspatial format (such as in propositions or lists of features)."[13] The abstract representation can then generate the pictorial representation.

> Image reconstruction would depend on the acquisition of abstract depictive knowledge in the first place and then on the ability to process that knowledge back into imaginal "copies" of

perceptual phenomena. That is, both processes of mental analysis and of mental synthesis are required: There is deconstruction and reconstruction. But this means that event knowledge is not represented in pictorial or analog form. (Foulkes, 1985, p. 158)

So this central issue is posed for Foulkes as for Neisser: If there are no mnemic copies, how does the abstract generate pictorial concrete representations? How are we to understand "mental synthesis" and "reconstruction?"

I think that Foulkes, like Neisser, does tend to waffle a bit on whether or not copies are available.

> What we must suppose, I think, is that there is modular memory—memory for the precise appearance, sound, affective, kinesthetic, etc. characteristics of life experiences—and that this memory, although we cannot consciously reflect on its knowledge, can be *used* in the service of symbolic processing activities. The knowledge in modular memory must be far more detailed than what we are ordinarily able to recall or to describe of the literal texture of what we've seen and heard and felt. (Foulkes, 1985, p. 176)

Precise and detailed memory of a literal texture surely sounds like the mnemic copies that Foulkes is at pains to deny.[14] For another example of waffling,

> There is not space here to consider later stages of dream production, in which imaginal production systems are recruited in the service of the evolving dream plan. Indeed, not much as yet is known about them. Presumably, the selection of lexical items activates processes of appearance generation, sound generation, and affect generation. As Freud (1900) observed, imaginal generation would be more successful for certain lexical items—concrete ones, for instance—than for others—abstract ones. But, by virtue of the prior selection of a narrative or perception-stimulating discourse plan, *most of the lexical input to the image generator already would be suitably concrete for visual depiction.* (Foulkes, 1982, p. 184, emphasis added)

But if the lexical input to the image generator is already "suitably concrete," then we are back to "precise and detailed memory of a literal texture" that serves as raw material for image generation, which sounds like Freud's compositional theory again, now translated into psycholinguistic terminology. But putting aside the waffling on mnemic copies, let's consider two possibilities for "synthesizing" images. The earlier Foulkes invokes Freud in an account based on "topographic regression."

4.4a The Topographic Regression Theory

Now Foulkes avoids dichotomizing imaging and waking perceiving, in line with the traditional view. Waking imaging is a weak form of dream perception for him (". . . the general rule is that our dream imagery is our most vivid imagery,")[15] and dreaming perception is phenomenologically equivalent to waking perception, a full-fledged "perceptual simulation,"[16] and so all come under the same theory. For later Neisser, as we saw, an image whether imagined or dreamed is the "inner aspect" of "unfulfilled perceptual readiness," and sharply distinguished from waking perception.[18] "Imagining and perceiving are fundamentally different," later Neisser says.[18]

Although Foulkes unites imaging with perception during dreaming and waking, against later Neisser, he quite agrees with him that the theory should not admit any representations in the form of mnemic copies. But he wants then to cure Neisser's difficulties by invoking the "topographic regression" notion of Freud:

> I am assuming an exact topographic inversion of waking and dreaming information processing, namely that the dream begins where waking stimulus comprehension ends, in meaning memory. (Foulkes, 1982, p. 175)

During waking, thought begins with a perceptual experience in consciousness and the direction of subsequent stimulus processing is "progressive." However in sleep,

> the perceptual and motor systems to the outside world are shut down, and system Cs primarily senses through elements derived

> from inner experience . . . the end product of the thought pro-
> cess is a sensory image which condenses a number of lines of
> thought emanating from different complexes of this sort [i.e.
> complexes "carrying Ucs meaning"] . . . Thus, sleeping thought
> *ends* where waking thought begins, with a percept which we
> believe to represent external reality. (Foulkes, 1978, p. 80, brac-
> kets added)

Thus Foulkes follows Freud in turning the waking model, as he says, "on its head."[19]

> We learn procedures, for instance, for transforming visually per-
> ceived stimuli into appropriate concepts and/or words. In the
> generation of mental imagery, that is, imagery experienced in the
> absence of correlative retinal stimulation, these procedures may
> be "topographically reversed." (Foulkes, 1982, p. 174)

There results " ' degeneration' of abstract verbal or spatial schemata into more literal perceptual constituents" and "information flowing 'back-ward' in sleep, resulting in 'sensory-like' images."[20] So we must see if "topographic reversal" can do the work of synthesizing the concrete per-ceptual images of dreams.

In topographic progression ("analysis," "deconstruction") we go from concrete waking experiences *to* the abstract representation. In topographic regression ("synthesis," "reconstruction") we are supposed to recover concrete waking experiences *from* the abstract representation. But the abstract representation is a universal that has indefinitely many instantiations; a particular instance cannot be recovered from it. We might go from a particular triangle to the concept of triangles, but then we cannot get back to that particular triangle or any particular triangle, except arbitrarily. The universal has no literal perceptual constituents, no non-abstract information that might "flow back" into sensory-like im-ages. It follows that construction cannot undo deconstruction. *Topo-graphic process as defined by Foulkes is not reversible.* Let's consider, then, a different approach by Foulkes to the problem of synthesizing the life-world of dreams.

4.4b Analysis-cum-Synthesis

Another method for forming the life-world—more congenial to cognitive science than topographic regression—is by first analyzing input and then synthesizing a product based on the results of analysis. Take production of the token 'A':

> Just as, in perceptual recognition, a rule might be, "if it has two lines at a 45° angle and a cross-bar, assign it the linguistic value "capital A", so, in image generation, a rule might be "create a pattern in which two lines intersect at a 45° angle and add a cross-bar." (Foulkes, 1982, p. 175)

No copies are involved in analysis-*cum*-synthesis; the analysis *abstracts* information from the copy level. The information abstracted then guides the synthesis. The analogy here is to computer graphics, but where an automated analysis of input plays the role of the computer artist.[21] The basic difficulty with the analysis-*cum*-synthesis machine account of dream world production has to do with where the graphics program comes from. To appreciate this difficulty, we need to consider the nature of neural codes, which has been greatly demystified by Clark.

The computational theory of mind implies that neural encodings have all the properties of a number system. Neural representations comprise an algebraic system.

> The visual system literally *measures* features of light and maps them into numeric codes. Those codes are numeric because they satisfy the postulates of elementary number theory, and are therefore isomorphic to rational numbers. (Clark, 1984, p. 3)

The distinction between numbers and tokens of numerals is important here.

> Note that the codes are *not* numbers (which are abstract entities and not neural states) nor do they necessarily name numbers (their interpretation is within vision and not within set theory).

The point is that the codes satisfy the logical relational structure defining numbers and hence provide a model for the rationals. (Clark, 1984, p. 7)

So neural encodings or "representations" are tokens of numerals (tokens of conventional symbols representing numbers), and computations over these representations exhibit all the structural properties of numerical computation. Neural encodings are thus numeric codes.

The graphics problem, then, is how to get from a numeric code to a pictorial representation. The neural encodings constitute an *uninterpreted* purely syntactic calculus. To say that the neural encoding is "of" two lines intersecting at a 45° angle connected by a crossbar *is already to interpret the code pictorially.* The problem for Foulkes—as for the computational theory of mind in general—is where the pictorial representation comes from (without invoking a *deus ex machina*). All the brain has is numeric codes, but somehow concrete life-worlds are produced. The brain encodes constant relations and invariant proportions as we walk around the table (4.3a), but the table *looks rectangular* to us. The brain contains a numeric code for a texture gradient, but *we see a certain depth of field.* An account of the mapping of numeric code onto the world concretely perceived is lacking.

In the case of computer graphics, the programmer plays the role of semantic interpreter and provides the mapping. The programmer sets up the machine's innards such that it can draw intersecting and connecting lines in various arrangements, can "create patterns," as Foulkes says. But these "patterns" are already pictorial, not purely syntactic. The machine's innards are set up such that the machine encoding of an input token 'A' will be fed into the graphics program which will end up drawing a token 'A'. Since the machine is perfectly coupled with its surrounding world—we see that whenever presented with an input 'A' the machine invariably produces an 'A'—we have the compelling illusion that the machine has the pictorial world on its own, forgetting that the programmer has set the whole thing up that way. The machine is confined to a purely syntactic domain, and that it produces something which concretely models the machine's surrounding is only because of external contrivance.

The synthesis side of analysis-*cum*-synthesis, then, collapses. Machines can't synthesize graphical worlds left to their own syntactical devices. The cognitivist account of dreaming life-world production requires a homunculus, or *deus ex machina,* or some ghost in the machine, for synthesis of a pictorial world to be accomplished. But if the dream life is generated neither by compositing mnemic copies nor by machine analysis-*cum*-synthesis, then just what non-dualistic mechanism might serve formative creativity in dreaming and waking? Is it even conceivable that there be such machines?

4.5 THE MACHINE BASIS OF FORMATIVE CREATIVITY: THE LEIBNIZ MACHINE

4.5a Introduction

The account of human beings developed in chapter three implies that there must be a proper machine—a "Leibniz machine," if you will, that deals in possible worlds—for these beings to supervene on. This machine's condition is methodologically solipsistic. It admits no copies of its surrounding and detects only whether or not its internally generated abstract specifications have been satisfied. Indeed, *the Leibniz machine contains all possibilities a priori.* The set of all possible worlds is in some sense originary to the Leibniz machine. This machine is able to produce a model of its surrounding by selection from its a priori plenum of possibilia. Formative creativity for the Leibniz machine is thus the process:

$$\text{a priori possibilia} \quad \xrightarrow{\text{by selection}} \quad \text{a posteriori existentia.}$$

Now it must be admitted that a "Leibniz machine" sounds strange. Surely it is not a computer, which we have been at pains to see is syntactically creative, not formatively creative, and thus the wrong kind of machine. "Please show me such a peculiar machine," the demand might be properly made. "An existence proof, if you please."

One goal of this section is to answer that demand, and show that evolution has indeed developed a very wet Leibniz machine in the immune system. Of course, it is the brain, not the immune system, that the present discussion requires to be at least in part a Leibniz machine. But Jerne (1967) has suggested that the brain functions analogously to the immune system, and Edelman has even attempted a brain model along those lines. (Both Jerne and Edelman won Nobel prizes for their work in immunology.) After all, the immune system has to recognize the surrounding antigen world, learn to expect what antigen the future might bring based on past experience, and produce antiworld and world models. So if the immune system is indeed a very wet Leibniz machine, then it is not so far-fetched to consider the possibility that the brain might be a wet one.

The second goal of this section is to consider a brain schematic which although admittedly speculative shows that the brain is at least *conceivable* as a Leibniz machine, thereby opening a door to the unknown. For all the present argument really requires, given that higher brain function is a virtual terra incognita, is that formatively creative machines not be utterly impossible. How the brain actually works will be told by utopian brain science. My claims are only that the brain must support formative creativity, per the argument of the first three chapters, that biological formatively creative machines do exist, and that a formatively creative brain machine is at least conceivable.

4.5b The Immune System[22]

The B lymphocytes of the immune system produce little pieces of flypaper called "antibodies" to which little potentially noxious antigen flies become stuck and are thereby removed from circulation. The sticking region on the antibody is called "paratope" and the matching region on antigen is called "epitope." Crudely speaking, the match is like key and lock, world and antiworld. (The immune system is indifferent whether the epitope/paratope fit is like key/lock or lock/key.) When the paratope displayed by a B cell is matched well enough, the B cell begins to secrete its antibody and to proliferate, forming a clone of genetically related cells, which secrete related antibodies. So the B cells produce an antiworld that models well enough the immune system's surrounding antigen world. When the antigen disappears, the matching B cells "remember" it, remaining ready for that antigen.

The little pieces of flypaper produced by the B cells may also stick together, since antibody also has antigenic properties. The antibody's epitope is called "idiotope." Let's consider what happens when the paratope, P_A, displayed by the B lymphocyte, B, is matched well enough by the epitope, E_A. Production of P_A is amplified. Now there is some other B cell, B_Y, displaying an idiotope, I_A, that is matched well enough by P_A. Production of I_A is amplified. But I_A is anti-antiworld, so I_A is world, equivalent to E_A. Thus depending on the antigen world that the immune system encounters, it produces a model antibody antiworld and also a model antibody world.

The immune system has *a priori* many millions, perhaps even billions, of different B cells, each displaying and secreting a slightly different antibody.[23] This immense a priori repertoire is generated by a confluence of genetic and random factors. The genome specifies only several hundreds of original B cells, but through gene splicing and recombination this original set is enormously diversified. Furthermore, when B cells proliferate, they mutate rapidly, so the cell clone further diversifies enormously. Because of these random factors, genetically identical individuals will have little overlap in their sets of B cells. Over the entire species, the immune systems generate the set of all possible antibody antiworlds and worlds, and each individual generates a representative subset of the set of all possible antibody antiworlds and worlds.

Since there is a corresponding set of all possible antigen worlds, there is potentially for each individual a many-to-one mapping of antigen onto antibody in the match. Given the contingent matches made as the immune system encounters its surrounding world, a subset of the representative subset of all possible antibody antiworlds is amplified, and then a subset of the representative subset of all possible antibody worlds is amplified. The end result is that the immune system brings forth from an a priori plenum antibody antiworlds and worlds that well enough model the surrounding antigen world.

So the immune system is a very wet monad. It generates a representative sample of all possibilities a priori (making notable use of random factors). It sets up specifications (conditions of satisfaction) at its interface with the surrounding world, and when satisfied well enough produces negative and positive models of the surrounding world by selective amplification from its a priori plenum. No copies of or building instructions from the surrounding world are required; the immune system is functionally windowless, registering only the impact of the match. The monadic immune system utilizes its own resources to create de novo by selective amplification its antiworld and world models. Its core processes are specifying, matching and producing.

The immune system is such a remarkable system, and its elucidation such a great achievement of science, that it is worth dwelling on its machine characteristics, bringing them into sharper focus by connecting to well-known systems that we more typically think of as machines. The next section compares the immune machine to a computer with a Newell architecture. We will see that B cells are like Newell "productions,"[24] except that B cells are a priori and productions a posteriori.

4.5c The Immune Machine and the Newell Computer Architecture

The working elements of the Newell architecture are called "productions." All productions act on a common memory, called the "workspace." Each production constantly surveys the entire workspace, looking for a certain pattern. When the requisite pattern is found in the workspace, then the production modifies it in some specific way. So the rule is: Whenever _____ is satisfied, perform _____.

> . . . each production acts on its own, when and where its private conditions are satisfied. . . . All communication and influence is via patterns in the common workspace—like anonymous "to whom it may concern" notices on a public bulletin board. Accordingly, overall direction emerges only as the net effect of many independent decisions. . . . (Haugeland, 1985, p. 158)

Programming a computer with a Newell Architecture is a matter of constructing productions; "the productions themselves are the program."[25]

The Newell architecture is nicely captured by Haugeland's metaphor of "Newell chefs," each of which is an expert at doing something effectively.

> For instance, one modest expert might look exclusively for a pint of whipping cream, flanked by a whisk and a cold copper bowl.

Unless and until that appears, he does nothing; but as soon as it does, he rushes over, whips the cream in the bowl and discards the whisk. Most such actions modify the patterns in the workspace, which may then "satisfy" some other specialist, such as the cake decorator, who has been waiting patiently for a bowl of whipped cream. And thus the processing continues. (Haugeland, 1985, p. 157)

Locations in the Newell workspace are content-addressable; locations are accessed not by the name of an address or by directions on how to get there, but by the pattern actually stored there. Furthermore, productions are *self-activating* in virtue of attaining satisfaction. In Turing, von Neumann and McCarthy architectures, by way of contrast, the units are ordered into operation by other units.

Now when the productions are activated, in virtue of being satisfied, they syntactically rearrange the satisfying pattern found in the workspace. But it would be equally feasible to have the production do its thing, whatever that happens to be, without making use of the pattern that satisfies it. The pattern that meets the production's conditions of satisfaction would function only to pick out that production for activation. So productions are a set of possible actions given satisfaction of certain conditions, and depending on what's in the workspace, certain actions are actually effected.

We can now see how the immune system's B cells are like Newell productions. The rule to the production, "whenever ____ is satisfied, produce ____," becomes the rule to the B cell: "whenever displayed antibody is matched well enough, produce antibody and more cells." But there is this major difference. The B cells are given by genetic and random factors a priori, providing all possibilities, and Newell productions are programmed in as needed a posteriori. Computers are empty, the contemporary *tabula rasa*. A computer with a Newell architecture is accordingly not a Leibniz machine. But the essential idea of the Newell production is relevant to the Leibniz machine: basic elements that abstractly specify, and when satisfied, do something (such as produce worlds).

We next want to consider if the brain might function along the lines of the immune system, looking over to the technology of *optical* information processing systems. Since this is a large topic that expands well beyond the scope of the present book, I present it here in a cursory but hopefully suggestive fashion.[26]

4.5d Optical Information Processing Systems

The contemporary "Turing's Man" looks over to the computer in attempting to fathom the brain's incredible complexity. I look instead to the new technology of optical information processing.[27] In this regard the popular imagination has been captured by a species of optical information processing called "holography." Holography produces images like photography but advances over photography in creating three-dimensional images. Perhaps the brain produces its images like holography produces an image from a hologram, the idea goes.[28] This fascination with holography has somewhat constricted the attention, which is properly directed towards the general category of optical information processing systems. Such systems can perform calculations, recognize, associate and mirror, as well as produce images.

In optical systems the information flows through filters. Coherent light diffracted from a source object is typically transformed before being inputed to the filter. This transformation is a Fourier transformation, and can be accomplished by passing the diffracted light through the proper lens. The output from the filter is in the transform domain, but a second Fourier transformation by a lens can convert it back to the domain of the object. The filter itself encodes a Fourier transform. The filter plays the functional role of the program in a computer, but it operates as an instantaneous whole rather than in a sequence of discrete steps.

The logic of optical information processing systems is fundamentally different from the logic of the computer. Yevick calls it a "Fourier logic" and Pietsch a "wavy logic," to be distinguished from the Boolean logic of computers. Whereas Boolean logic is based on a binary number system—0 and 1 suffice—Fourier logic requires imaginary numbers (complex numbers of the form a+bi). What essentially characterizes Fourier logic, I think, is that the basic operations are with and on wholes rather than strings of discrete elements. This holistic logic has its own concepts of identity, equality, inclusion and association, as Yevick discusses.

Looking back to the brain from the standpoint of optical systems, the implication is that the natural mathematical description of brain functioning requires complex numbers. The complexity of what needs to be expressed mathematically is staggering. There are roughly 10^{10} neurons in the brain and 10^{14} synaptic connections between neurons (including synapses a neuron makes with itself). The whole richly interconnected system is in continuous flux. This fluctuating whole pattern can be conceived of as if waves were coming together moment-to-moment so as to form a complicated interference pattern. (This idea apparently originated with Lashley (1929).) The mathematical description of brain functioning does not necessarily require the Fourier transform but may entail the La Place transform, spinors or whatever. The mathematical formalism for representing such a system, however, would naturally utilize complex numbers for wave amplitude and phase representation.

Now holography is a special version of an optical system; the hologram is a kind of filter. The hologram can be constructed as follows. A laser beam is split in two. One component is diffracted from the object to be imaged and then rejoins the other component. But the intersecting waves now variously reinforce and cancel each other ("superposition") so as to form an interference pattern. This resulting interference pattern is recorded on a photographic negative, and called a hologram. The hologram shows no image to gross inspection, unlike an ordinary photographic negative, and on finer inspection shows only complicated patterns of wave interference.

Now suppose the hologram is inserted as a filter in the optical information processing system, and the input is the original laser beam. The output from the filter is the image of the object. This process is called holographic image reproduction. Now let the input be from the object, or something similar to the object, and the output is the coherent light source. Here there is recognition, a matching of input and filter; the intensity of the output is proportional to the similarity, i.e. a correlation is computed. Image reproduction from the filter does not necessarily require specific input. The image encoded to the filter by Fourier transformation can be recovered from the filter by inverse Fourier transformation. Another unique property of the hologram is that if we take just a piece of it and use the piece as an optical filter, still the image of the entire object can be reproduced. (Only a piece of the object can be reproduced from a piece of an ordinary photographic negative. When the piece of the hologram becomes too small, the image becomes blurred and the window of observation narrows.) Thus the whole is in each piece of the hologram—the one in the many—which is an ideal setup for parallel processing.

Bohm's terminology is very useful here. The order of the source object is said to be "enfolded" or "implicated" to the hologram, and given the proper input, or by inverse Fourier transformation, can be "unfolded" or "explicated" from the hologram. The implicate order is an entirely new conception of order, Bohm brings out, quite different from classical optics whose order is limited to the explicate order with its Cartesian coordinates.

A major limitation of holography, it should be noted, is that the hologram is so static. Like the ordinary photographic negative, the hologram must be "developed," and once developed it is rigidly fixed. But other kinds of materials than light sensitive film emulsion (e.g. liquid crystals) can be used that allow the filter to be modulated in real time.[27] Real time hybrid optical/digital systems have been described.[28]

A refinement of the optical filter, constructed from more complicated transformations, is crucial to the present discussion. Cavanagh has shown that it is possible to construct a recognition filter whose response is invariant to the size, location and orientation of the object to be recognized, and is also sensitive to similarity. Such a filter enfolds not the image of an object but has the remarkable property of enfolding the *eidos* of an object; it encodes abstract specifications, and the filter can be made to ring its satisfaction to criterion when matched by input. (Note that the connotation of a filter as something information is "passed through" drops away here; this "filter" is a resonator.)

Suppose we construct an *eidos*-filter for the letter 'H'. Then the filter recognizes—rings its satisfaction—whatever the size, location or orientation of an 'H' source of input and whatever the type font. We might construct an *eidos*-filter for each letter of the alphabet. Now suppose we constructed a set of filters for size, location and orientation, and further constructed a set of filters for the basic elements from which the letter pattern is formed. (The letter H is standardly composed of continuous straight lines, but it might also be composed of dots arranged in lines, or continuously squiggly lines, or narrow rectangles, etc.)

Given this array of filters—a plenum of possibilia for the alphabet—

then the suitably transformed input from any letter—whatever its size, location, orientation or basic elements—would make some matches. The set of filters matched might then reproduce the input by inverse Fourier transformation. These filters are like Newell productions: Whichever filter specs are matched by input, inversely Fourier transform them— which produces an image of input. (Again, nothing is passed through the matched filter on this conception; the filter unfolds enfolded order when matched.)

But the alphabet reproduction machine just described is not a Leibniz machine. The optical information processing system, like the computer, is an empty *tabula rasa* device. The optical programmer constructs a filter rather than an algorithm, as a computer programmer does, but still has to load it into the otherwise vacant machine. The brain required by the present argument, however, is a priori full with possibility, like the immune system. Here the filters are not put into the wet machine by an external *deus ex machina* but are always already inherent to the machine, given by the genome selected in evolution.

4.5e The Brain as Leibniz Machine

Let's consider a large set of "hyperneurons," idealized entities each conceived of as a richly interconnected group of neurons. A hyperneuron functions equivalently to a B cell or Newell production. It has conditions, and when satisfied, produces something, in this case a model of the surrounding world.

Let's think of the hyperneuron as displaying an interference pattern that "enfolds" specifications, like an image is enfolded to a hologram. We understand this to mean that the hyperneuron's codings satisfy the logical relational structure defining *complex numbers*, not rational numbers, and provide a model of a domain with real and imaginary components. The pattern of the hyperneuron enfolds the same specifications to small regions of the hyperneuron, just as in holography the order of a concrete token is enfolded to small regions of a hologram. The hyperneuron is functionally a matched filter. There are two kinds of input to the hyperneuron. *Tuning input* alters the hyperneuron's specifications. *Sensory input* is matched to the hyperneuron's specifications. Sensory input also modulates the tuning input.

When the hyperneuron's specifications are satisfied well enough by the sensory input pattern, a region of the hyperneuron is inversely Fourier transformed, which unfolds the enfolded order and the hyperneuron outputs a pattern that well enough models the sensory input pattern. Thus a certain token 'A' as input pattern will match the hyperneuron that encodes (enfolds) the universal A and also match the hyperneurons that specify the concrete properties of the token (its size, orientation, location, and kind of element). The hyperneurons satisfied are activated for production, and a model 'A' produced by inverse Fourier transformation. In effect, hyperneuronal satisfaction results in hyperneuronal autotransformation that unfolds enfolded order.

The analogy between B cell and hyperneuron is quite close. A perfect match between the sensory input pattern and the hyperneuron's pattern occurs when the latter is the complex conjugate of the former. The hyperneurons are thus a kind of "antiworld," like paratope to epitope, but in a world domain that admits imaginary values. Inverse Fourier transformation results in a world that models well enough the world source of input, like the idiotope world well models the epitope world.

We can conceive of a large set of hyperneurons being set up a priori by a confluence of genetic and random factors, a set that might match well enough *whatever* the input pattern might be. Hyperneurons might be much more flexible than B cells, and improve their match to an input pattern with continued experience, as in Grossberg's concept of "adaptive resonance." (Actually the immune system is flexible, but relatively slowly. Because of high mutation rates, the clone of B cells deriving from a matched B cell diverges. Some member of the clone will better match antigen and be selectively amplified. Thus the immune antiworld and world is over time fine-tuned to the antigen world.) Some hyperneurons might have specifications well defined by the genome, rather than subject to random factors. Thus the gosling would have genetically given hyperneurons specifying "large moving objects" and the infant would have hyperneurons specifying "faces." Through something like adaptive resonance during a critical period of development, the gosling's hyperneurons typically become fine-tuned to mother goose and the infant's hyperneurons to mama.[29]

Thus the hyperneuron's specifications comprise an a priori set of possible worlds for the species, modifiable through experience, and modulated in accordance with the current environmental and intentional situation. When satisfied well enough by the input pattern, a good enough model of the input pattern is produced by transformation of the hyperneuronal specifications.

Note that the graphics problem discussed in 4.4b does not arise here. There is no a posteriori instructed synthesis. Instead world is *de facto* enfolded originally through genetic and random factors, modified by adaptive resonance a posteriori, and continually intentionally tuned ("cognitively penetrated") and environmentally modulated. World production is not by instructed synthesis but by selective unfolding from the a priori plenum of hyperneuronal possibilia in virtue of the match. Because the numeric codes are isomorphic to complex numbers rather than rational numbers, they are able to enfold pictorial representations, and pictorial representations can be unfolded from them. In effect, the mapping of numeric codes onto pictorial representations is by autotransformations.

The idealized hyperneurons just described comprise the active elements of a Leibniz machine. World models are produced without benefit of copies of the world or instructions from the world; they are created formatively. Certain a priori specifications within the machine are satisfied by the world and then transformed to a good enough world model. All possibilities are always already within the machine, and the model of the surrounding is realized from these possibilities.

4.5f Comment

Since my speculation about brain functioning may bother those enamoured of bench science, something more needs to be said by way of justification. I am approaching the brain from a radically different direction—reflexively—compared to empirical brain science. I am saying that we human beings are formatively creative (by the arguments of the first three chapters) and so the brain *has* to support formative creativity. This is the same line taken by Dreyfus in his seminal *What computers can't do.* (See also the recent *Mind over machine* by Dreyfus and Dreyfus.) Dreyfus argues in effect that computers can't do what we human beings can do, and so the brain can't be a wet computer. This implies that there must be some other kind of machine that *can* do what human beings can. Dreyfus even points towards holographic brain theory for a possible alternative.

This peculiar approach to the brain functioning—from an account of human capabilities to the kind of machine there would have to be for humans to have such capabilities—is in a certain sense transcendental in spirit. "Transcendental" refers to the condition for the possibility of mind, or consciousness, or being, or however the human being is taken. (Kant, Husserl and Heidegger are the great masters of the transcendental approach.) The present transcendental question is: What is the condition for the possibility of our formative creativity? We see from reflection on our dreaming and waking lives that we are formatively creative, and the condition for the possibility of formative creativity is a brain machine—which is not computer-like—upon which formative creativity might supervene.

The requisite machine—which I have dubbed the "Leibniz machine"—belongs to an equivalence class of which there is at least one (very wet) member, viz. the immune system. The requirements on such a machine are bizarre. All possible worlds must be a priori to the machine. The actual world is produced from this plenum of possibilia, selected by input and intention. No copy of the input is required, since all worlds always already lie within the machine.

Just how the brain might provide the supervenience base for formative creativity is quite unknown. Our scientific knowledge of the brain is spectacular at lower levels and undeveloped at the highest level. There is no evidence that the brain is computer-like at its highest level of functioning; the computer is just the model that contemporary Turing's man finds compelling. What I have been about here is seeing if it is a least conceivable that the brain might be a wet Leibniz machine. In this regard I have turned to optical information processing systems, but other models are available.[30]

My basic idea is that the possible worlds do "exist," but as an enfolded order. Since Bohm, it is clear that existence has two modes: enfolded and unfolded, whereas formerly only unfolded existence was admitted. But this opens the way to a new notion of possibility: *Possibility is implicate existence.* Actuality depends on a process of unfolding enfolded order to explicate existence.

The brain notion is that sets of richly interconnected neurons ("hyperneurons") be thought of as (mathematically) complex, continuously tunable filters on input that enfold possible worlds. There is a primitive set of filters given a priori by a confluence of genetic and random factors, and enriched by experience. Properly speaking, the plenum of possibilia is restricted—restricted to universal human possibilia and further restricted by individual human experience. Such filters have a remarkable second function in addition to enfolding possible worlds: They set up continuously changing abstract specifications on their input. Those filters whose conditions of satisfaction are met to criterion are selected and their enfolded orders unfolded as an explicate world. Such a brain would be a wet Leibniz machine and could provide a supervenience basis for our formative creativity. How the brain actually supports our formative creativity will be decided by utopian brain science.

4.6 SUMMARY

The cognitive approach to dreaming attempts to account for formation of the dreaming life-world without making use of Freud's mnemic copies (although some waffling can be detected). The key idea, *pace* Foulkes (1985), is that of analysis-*cum*-synthesis by a computer-like brain, where the results of analysis instruct the synthesis. However, synthesis of concrete pictorial life-worlds goes beyond the resources of a purely syntactical machine like a computer. An external semantically capable interpreter is always required to set the machine graphics up so that the machine's numeric codes will produce pictorial world models. Foulkes' account of dream world production is forced to rely on a *deus ex machina*.

The prospects for a monadic possible worlds machine with a capacity for formative creativity was considered. The immune system is just such a Leibniz machine. A brain schematic (akin to optical information processors) is conceivable that is comparable to the immune system. Machines that are formatively creative thus both biologically exist and are conceivable. The requirement that a monadic being supervene on a machine that supports formative creativity does not in principle constrain the account developed in the first three chapters, since there are in fact prospects for a monadic brain machine.

Chapter Five

The Dream
as Oracle

*Think only of the mysteries; mystery is all
that matters.* Carlos Castaneda, The fire
from within (1984, p. 283)

*. . . the symbol in the dream has more the
value of a parable: it does not conceal, it
teaches.* C.G. Jung, "The structure and
dynamics of the psyche" (1960, p. 246)

5.1 INTRODUCTION

A topic ignored thus far in my dream discussions is a certain "folk understanding" of dreams, deeply entrenched beliefs outside of the scientific and philosophical tradition, that attribute to dreams a mysterious oracular power and intelligence. Jung has led the way in appreciating the oracular view of dreams as reflecting essentially the transpersonal wisdom of a *universal* unconscious, in stark contrast to the Freudian view that dreams distort the instinctual cravings of a personal unconscious. Jung's idea is that in dreaming we are in touch with a spirit beyond empirical science, something that transcends our personal selves. Our dreams give profound advice; we should "listen" to our dreams as to oracles, because wisdom is contained there. This is a "deeper" wisdom than we ordinarily know, and so we may profitably meditate upon our dreams. It is a deep current within us, even a biological wisdom selected in evolution, that expresses itself most clearly in dreams, when our daytime chatter ceases under the condition of sleep.

The dream is quite as important for Jung as it is for Freud, for in dreams we can discern the core universal unconscious operations:

> Because dreams are the most common and most normal expression of the unconscious psyche, they provide the bulk of the material for its investigation. (Jung, 1974, p. 73)

The dream can be a clear and numinous expression of the "archetypes" which are at the heart of Jung's theory. So dreams are Jung's *via regia* to the truly "objective mind," the "collective unconscious," with its transpersonal archetypal wisdom. Before discussing the ways in which dreams are wise, something must be said of the archetypes.[1]

5.2 THE ARCHETYPES

The archetypes are "universal structures within the human mind."[2] These universal structures are a priori and abstract. It is true that Jung often talks about archetypes as if they were concrete images, but to be consistent, the images must be conceived of as *expressions* of the archetypes. Archetypal expressions are to be understood as

> specific forms and groups of images which occur not only at all times and in all places but also in individual dreams, fantasies, visions, and delusional ideas. Their frequent appearance in individual case material, as well as their universal distribution, prove that the human psyche is unique and subjective or personal only in part, and for the rest is collective and objective. (Jung, 1960, p. 291)

As a priori and abstract, archetypes are Kantian and Platonic in philosophical spirit. But the archetypes have biological underpinnings for Jung, as Stevens brings out.

Archetypes are biological in the sense that they are *predispositions* inherited in evolution. The evolving wisdom of the species is conserved in the genome (the total genetic make-up of the individual organism). The archetypal genes are realized as "predispositions for perceiving, feeling, behaving and conceptualizing in specific ways."[3] Put in existential terms, the archetypes are inherited tendencies towards ways of being in the world, Dasein's genetically given a priori horizon.

To illustrate, we are biologically predisposed to expect nurturing ("mothering"), to perceive (pick up) nurturing activities when present, and to have a particular constellation of feelings, behaviors and cognitions when the nurturing expectation is met. This predispostion, already present in the newborn and continuing throughout life, is the archetype "Good Great Mother." (Note how this label falsely suggests an image rather than a predisposition.) This way of being which is universal to the human species is matched by the person in the primal caretaking relationship to the infant. The primal nurturer is

> *there*—to constellate in human form the 'Great Good Mother', she who nurtures, warms, grants security, and who alone makes possible the continuance of life. (Stevens, 1983, p. 66)

There is also a "Terrible Great Mother," complementary to the Good Great Mother, which is also a universal predisposition.[4] The mother-infant dyad thus comprises a dynamic reciprocity between the archetypal predispositions and the nurturer.

There are as many archetypes as there are typical human situations that characterize the life cycle. That is, the archetypes are genetically given readinesses for the average expectable range of human experiences, the predispositions that have been selected in evolution *because they have been successful for social humankind.* The archetypes accordingly comprise the unconscious collective wisdom of the species.

5.3 ARCHETYPE AND DREAM

The relationship between the archetypes and dreams is that dreams *may* be expressions of the archetypes of the universal collective unconscious. Ordinary dreams ("little dreams") express the personal unconscious that characterizes a particular individual, but certain evocative, numinous dreams ("big dreams") express the collective unconscious. *Archetypal predispositions are thus expressed in dream images.*

Dream interpretation attempts to translate back from the archetypal expressions of the dream to the deep archetypal structures that generated the surface expressions.[5] Dream interpretation has a formal significance, since it unveils universal abstract a priori structures. It also has a personal significance, in that dream hermeneutics brings out archetypal wisdom for the benefit of the dreamer:

> The dream uses collective figures because it has to express an eternal human problem that repeats itself endlessly, and not just a disturbance of personal balance. (Jung, 1960, p. 292)

Thus the archetypes are relevant to the basic existential issues that confront humankind throughout the life cycle. Universal problems use universal symbols.

It should not be thought that the clinical value of Jungian dream hermeneutics is purely intellectual. The archetypal expressions are after all vitally *experienced.* The archetypes are lived out in a profoundly emotional way, as a way of being in the dream world. In living out the expression of the archetypal structure while dreaming, one comes into intimate contact with the collective unconscious.

Now Foulkes has criticized the idea so fundamental to Jung (and of course Freud) that dreams express meaning.[6] Foulkes says that "the dream narrative is not a translated message"[7] and that "the dream narrative does not contain encoded meanings."[8] The notion of a universal unconscious teaching through the dream narrative and images is plain ridiculous in Foulkes' eyes. There is no wisdom expressed in dreams that we might translate. So,

> what's sought in dream interpretation doesn't exist, ... there's no more underlying meaning in dreams than there are angels who might sit on the head of a pin. (Foulkes, 1985, p. 164)

Although Foulkes comes on very strong on this point, when looked at more closely his position is actually quite moderate. He means to say that there is no *deliberate intent* of an underlying purposive intelligence to send a message. But there are still "indicative meanings"[9] in dreams, "*signs* of the mind and thus the character of the person who dreamed it."[10]

> Thus, it is no mistake to assume that dreams are a potential source of information about the individual personality and about human nature. (Foulkes, 1985, p. 204)

Although Jung talks—as do clinicians in general—as if there is semantic intent on the part of the unconscious, there is no difficulty, and nothing lost, in seeing archetypal expressions as indicative meanings.

In terms of our previous discussions, the archetypes can be conceived of as genetically determined tunings of filters on input, filter settings selected in evolution and thereby adaptive ("wise"). During waking, input dominates the operative filters, picking out those that match input's vicissitudes, but during dreaming, the filters escape input's hegemony, and the genetically determined archetypal filter settings become operative, formatively creating life-worlds. We can then interpret back from the dream to the tuned filter's "indicative meanings."

5.4 THE LITTLE DREAM

Jung differs from Freud not only in his conception of the universal unconscious, but in his concept of the personal unconscious, and accordingly in his approach to the little dream. Jung's general approach to dreams is much less "scientific," less medical, and more spiritual, than that of Freud.[11] Whereas the psychic forces that Freud wrote about in his dream book were developed within a nineteenth century Helmholtzian biophysical framework (pre-relativity and quantum theory), Jung's writing has a much more contemporary "holistic," transpersonal, and mystical ring to it:

> But since everything living strives for wholeness, the inevitable one-sidedness of our conscious life is continually being corrected

and compensated by the universal human being in us, whose
goal is the ultimate integration of conscious and unconscious, or
better, the assimilation of the ego to a wider personality. (Jung,
1960, p. 292)

The psyche for Jung is self-regulating, self-restoring. Although Jung well
appreciates the dark side of the mind, Jung also trusts the psyche, whose
purposes he sees as health-promoting, whereas for Freud the psyche,
under the hegemony of dark unconscious wish and defense, is pres-
sured, conflicted, ill at ease.

Jung recognizes a number of dream functions but especially emphasizes that dreams *compensate* for waking, bring a better balance to the
mental life.

I believe it is true that all dreams are compensatory to the
content of consciousness . . . dreams contribute to the self-regulation of the psyche by automatically bringing up everything that
is repressed or neglected or unknown . . . (Jung, 1960, p. 25.)

Dreams, I maintain, are compensatory to the conscious situation
of the moment. (Jung, 1960, p. 252)

When the conscious attitudes deviate in a way that threatens the vital
needs of an individual, dreams occur with a strongly contrasting, purposive content. Dreams accordingly express self-regulation of the psyche. The dream compensates by filling out the whole picture.

The unconscious is the unknown at any given moment so it is
not surprising that dreams add to the conscious psychological
situation of the moment all those aspects which are essential for
a totally different point of view. It is evident that this function of
dreams amounts to a psychological adjustment, a compensation
absolutely necessary for properly balanced action. In a conscious
process of reflection it is essential that, so far as possible, we
should realize all the aspects and consequences of a problem in
order to find the right solution. This process is continued automatically in the more or less unconscious state of sleep, where,
as experience seems to show, all those aspects occur to the dreamer (at least by way of allusion) that during the day were insuf-

ficiently appreciated or even totally ignored—in other words, were comparatively unconscious. (Jung, 1960, p. 245)

The compensatory function shows the dreamer alternatives that were not apparent during waking:

If a dream shows me what sort of mistake I am making, it gives me an opportunity to correct my attitude, which is always an advantage. (Jung, 1960, p. 269)

So the dream reveals a creative intelligence at work.

Jung distinguishes the compensatory function of dreams from their "prospective function." Rather than being a purposive self-regulation, the prospective function is

an anticipation in the unconscious of future conscious achievements, something like a preliminary exercise or sketch, or a plan roughed out in advance. Its symbolic content sometimes outlines the solution of a conflict. (Jung, 1960, p. 255)

These dreams are not literal prophecies of what will happen but insightful plans for achieving some desirable state of affairs. The prospective function, too, reflects the health-promoting nature of dreams, the creative intelligence of the mind during REM sleep.

In the health-promoting compensatory and prospective functions of dreams, Jung thus formalizes the folk understanding of the dream as oracle. Jung of course far surpasses the folk understanding in the richness of his theory.

5.5 AN ILLUSTRATION OF THE ORACULAR FUNCTION*

I illustrate the oracular function of dreams as follows. A few days after my wife has been diagnosed as having breast cancer I have the following dream which grabs my attention, unlike the ordinary dream

*Betty Smith, faculty member at the C.G. Jung Institute of Los Angeles, worked with me on this dream and brought out an archetypal interpretation of it.

which quickly slips away from my grasp. We immediately know that such dreams are important, are "big dreams" as Jung says, even though their significance is obscure.

> I am walking through a field. A snake starts up out of the ground to my right some feet away and moves swiftly towards my left and into the open front door of a house. The snake has a peculiar pink-orange color, but even more fantastic, its movement is one of energetic bouncing, in a succession of swift, sinuous bounces, into the house. The house belongs to friends, the "Zs."

This dream seems transparent to me on waking reflection. The snake is a cancer that I wish onto someone else. The Zs have young children, like we do, so Mrs. Z stands in for my wife. Both snakes and cancers are fearful objects to me, adventitious killers. Then I realize that the setting of the dream is nothing like the setting in which the Zs live. The house and the field are actually elsewhere and I regard the lady of that house much more ambivalently than Mrs. Z. Clearly, I was wishing the cancer away on someone I didn't like that much. I am indeed always highly wary of snakes at that person's house for I have seen many while walking the fields. As a true snake-phobic, the snake's unexpected strike is for me a perfect symbol of an unexpectedly diagnosed cancer.

It had happened, furthermore, that a snake had briefly been in my consciousness earlier that evening during a film, John Weir's "The Last Wave", providing thereby a "day residue." The closing scenes of the film were very dark and somewhat confusing. At one point the protagonist had said something about snakes, and I had tried to see them, but could not pick them out. (My snake intention did not obtain its conditions of satisfaction.) The color pink-orange, too, was something I had failed to pick out the preceding day. While passing through the hospital cafeteria just before lunch closing, I commented that I didn't see much there and my companion pointed to a tray of salmon in the back of the hot area that I had missed. I had briefly glanced at the pink-orangey salmon thus pointed out, momentarily startled that I had not noticed it, and then had passed on. So both the snake and its color alluded to my failure to pick something out, a failure which was very much in my consciousness. With me for several days had been the feeling of painful self-reproach that I had failed to pick up the tumor, and my mind flagged certain trivial events of the day that also fulfilled the concept of "failing to pick up." Mental operations present at the time of these adventitious events (seeing the salmon color, trying to see a snake) became reoperative during REM sleep and generated the pink-orangey snake, as discussed in the first three chapters.

The other remarkable feature of the snake—its bouncing yet snake-like movements—yields few associations, as I continue to reflect on the dream. I think about this dream and even tell it to a few people, as I struggle to regain my emotional balance under the trauma of my wife's cancer, but the best I can come up with is Tigger, a character in Winnie the Pooh, who bounces a lot. The association to Tigger feels forced and unsatisfactory; there is a certain opacity to the central dream feature of bouncing.

A little over a week later one of the twins, almost four years old, seeks me out and says she wants to tell me a dream. This occurs on awakening in the morning the day after her mother returned home from surgery. She has never sought me out to tell a dream before, although I have on occasion asked her (and her twin) about dreams, but not for months. Their previous dream reports had not sounded very dream-like to me, but were something like stories they had been read. I had thought they probably did not yet have well-formed dreams. But this one immediately impresses me as dream-like. (Her mother reports another recent description by this child that sounded dream-like.)

A man pushed down the door by the windows [which is her outside door]. Then he (bp)ounced.

I hear her say "pounced" (a word she knows) and so I say, "Pounced! Were you scared when the man pounced on you?" "No, I was not scared," she says. "But if the man pounced on you, how come you weren't scared?" I persist, since the dream sounded scary to me, and it would not be surprising if the child had a nightmare given the circumstances of her mother's breast surgery. "Bounced," she corrects me determinedly. "Bounced and bounced and bounced."

I am quite astonished by the dream she confides before running off, which immediately reminds me of and seems to continue my own dream. Now she is in the house of my dream, where something enters and forcefully bounces. But she is not scared. Nor am I scared of the snake in my dream, I now realize, unlike my usual great anxiety about them. Furthermore, I was quite unconcerned for the occupants of the house. The snake bouncing into the house was just the fact, just a powerful, awesome force at play. I indeed had felt quite secure in my snake dream, like my daughter in hers.

Suddenly the dream as oracle becomes transparent to me. I have been very depressed, feeling helpless and hopeless, over our situation. The cancer has turned out to be highly malignant and has spread to the lymph nodes. Indeed, we have just had a "heavy discussion" about the whole thing, at the very time that my daughter was presumably in REM sleep and dreaming. My wife, in contrast to me, is totally confident that she will survive the cancer. She has mobilized all her forces, natural and social, to face six months of chemotherapy at three week intervals. I on the other hand feel overwhelmed and unequal to the challenge. The chemotherapy seems like six months of pure horror, a continuous *poisoning* of the body. The dream, however, is pointing out a more healthy possibility, that faces lifes without fear. My perception of our life situation is quickly transformed. I see the chemotherapy "poisonings" every three weeks as a series of bounces through sickness and relative well-being, rather than as an unmitigated horror.

Furthermore, the snake is not just something terrible that I wish away from my family onto others. It is also the powerful vital chemotherapy, the periodic poison that cures. I convey this to my wife, and through the dream images of my daughter and myself we together see the task facing us with greater clarity. Most remarkably, my depression lifts and I feel again fluid and buoyant. For the first time I apprehend powerful forces at work, salutary forces, which I have completely neglected in my depressed waking life, and so my situation is seen in a more balanced way. As Castaneda's "don Juan" might say, my "gap" which has been opened by the trauma of my wife's cancer closes up, and I am once again shakily "on the path." Jung too notes the sometimes salutary effect of dreams.

But anyone sufficiently interested in the dream problem cannot have failed to observe that dreams also have a continuity *for-*

wards—if such an expression be permitted—since dreams occasionally exert a remarkable influence on the conscious mental life even of persons who cannot be considered superstitious or particularly abnormal. These after-effects consist mostly in more or less distinct alterations of mood. (Jung, 1960, p. 238)

The meaning of the association to Tigger now opens up, a meaning I had resisted and discounted. The resilient Tigger after all bounces all the time—that is central to rabbit's complaint against him in the Winnie the Pooh story I read to the twins. And Tigger does have an orangy color in the book, reminiscent of the snake's color. As the story goes, rabbit wants to lose Tigger in the woods, and so teach him humility. But rabbit himself gets frightfully lost, and Tigger has to rescue him and guide him home. The "Tigger-snake" is thus a helpful guide, starting up from the unconscious to restore me to security. My dream is positive, compensating for my depressed waking state, and opening up new waking possibilities.

5.6 DISCUSSION

One might object, of course, that the oracular reading of the dream is quite arbitrary. In an alternative, more psychoanalytic interpretation, I wish the poisonous cancer on someone else . . . The snake is the destructive phallus; its bounces are coital motions . . . My defenses are good enough that I feel no anxiety . . . By what right do I take this dream as an oracle pointing out my "proper path" rather than an expression of unconscious wish and defense per Freud?

It must be conceded that there is nothing absolute about the oracular understanding of dreams vs. the psychoanalytic understanding of dreams, or any other understanding for that matter. Both interpretations have a certain validity. What is confusing is that the two interpretations run together. To see this, note that what changes in going from the psychoanalytic to the oracular interpretation of my dream is the snake symbol. In the psychoanalytic frame, the snake is the cancer. In the oracular frame, the snake is the chemotherapy that poisons the cancer, a vital, salutary, periodic (bouncing) force. So the two dream interpretations are true alternatives. The dream symbol is not like a rebus, as

Freud thought, but like an ambiguous figure (e.g. like the Necker cube or the duck-rabbit), in which the figure looks one way and then another. Indeed, the two interpretations represent two sides of me—the weak, frightened, paranoid side, and the strong, confident, healthy side. Under the conditions of REM sleep, the rules of both these sides (among others) become operative, and generate a compromise dreaming life-world that is like an ambiguous figure, that can be interpreted first one way and then another, back and forth. The two sets of rules are deep currents within me, expressing themselves in my dreams. The shadow current unexpressed in waking emerges in dreaming, and so the dream offers a more complete view of my true potential.

Seeing the two alternative interpretations of my dream, I have a choice, rather than being lost in (held fascinated by) the depressive description. I can live in accordance with my weak self or my strong self. The alternatives are displayed there in the oracular dream; my life-situation, my existential dilemma, is brought into high resolution. (Not that I have been completely unconscious of the issue, but only that I have no clarity regarding the issue and in my depression see no possibilities for choice.) During REM sleep, when my waking chatter ceases, my various ways of Being become operative and are expressed in the life-world they generate. The oracular dream thus points to different possible but neglected ways of Being, by virtue of being the ambiguous compromise product of the sets of rules governing those ways of Being. Seeing these possibilities with clarity, the choice is mine.

My discussion of the dream thus far has been more Jungian in spirit than Freudian, in that I have emphasized the healthy forces at work in my dream life. In Jungian terms the positive construal of chemotherapy present in the dream "compensates" for my overly negative and depressed waking construal. There is a "prospective" function as well, in that a rough plan takes shape for coping with the next six months, a preparation for "psychological bouncing" attuned to the chemotherapy. There are, however, different emphases in the present understanding of dreams compared to Jung, emphases more aligned in spirit to Freud.

Jung sees the unconscious as purposive, as actively working to promote balanced health by compensation of waking over-involvements and by insightful planning. This occurs "automatically," Jung says, but this automaticity is not truly mechanistic, not blind forces at work for Jung. The unconscious for Jung is actively intelligent, an intelligence automatically brought to bear upon "the conscious situation of the moment."

In contrast, on my view there is no shadow intelligence in the unconscious that operates in dreams. Instead sets of rules (including rules from the collective unconscious) become operative and generate *de novo* a dream that is like an ambiguous figure, encompassing both salutary and unsalutary ways of Being. The condition of REM sleep frees *all* of our ways of Being to become operative, whereas during waking there is intense attachment to one way of Being, so that alternatives are not available. The dream does not compensate for waking excess but expresses a more balanced presentation of all our possible ways of Being. Just as in the ambiguous figure I alternate between seeing a duck and then a rabbit, I discern in my dream alternative interpretations of the snake as death-producing and life-giving. But whatever the differences from Jung, I follow him in seeing the dream as functionally teaching rather than concealing.

In my discussion of the oracular dream so far, the oracular function is something quite rational. The oracle turns out to be wholly natural forces at play, rather than something that lies outside of the nomological net of science. Mystery enters, however, in the claim that my daughter completes my dream, at the very acme of my existential crisis, that her dream smoothly picks up where my dream leaves off, and highlights the very place where my dream is opaque. This smacks of the occult. It is something akin to what Castaneda calls *"dreaming* together."[12]

This mystery might be avoided by saying that it was just a chance happening that the dream-gift she brought to me entailed something bouncing in her room. It might be said that the only real connection between my daughter's dream and mine is the connection that *I* draw, draw through some dim-witted fascination with mystery, sorcery, Indians and the whole occult California sixties bouillabaisse in which my thoughts first fermented. It must be admitted that as human beings, we do have an extraordinary ability to make meaningful connections.

Alternatively, we may take the seeming connection between her dream and mine at face value. Her dream mysteriously continues mine, and brings to expression oracular knowledge. As "don Juan" says

> The world is a mystery. This, what you're looking at, is not all
> there is to it. There is much more to the world, so much more,
> in fact, that it is endless. So when you're trying to figure it out,
> all you're really doing is trying to make the world familiar. (Cas-
> taneda, 1973, p. 168)

Thus explanation treats out insecurity in the face of the uncanny. But my
daughter's continuing my dream is not the only thing touched by mystery. An archetype from the collective unconscious appears in my
dream.

5.7 AN ARCHETYPAL VIEW

It is at time of life crisis, Jung emphasized, when fundamental existential issues are raised, that archetypal expressions break through into
the dream life from the collective unconscious, like the snake starts up in
the field of my dream.

Jung thought that snakes symbolize primitive brain functioning, the
reptilian brain that persists at the core of the mammalian brain.

> The lower vertebrates have from earliest times been favourite
> symbols of the collective psychic substratum (higher vertebrates
> symbolize mainly affects), which is localized anatomically in the
> subcortical centres, the cerebellum and the spinal cord. These
> organs constitute the snake. Snake dreams usually occur, there-
> fore, when the conscious mind is deviating from its instinctual
> basis. (Stevens, 1983, p. 269)

Thus my snake dream emerges in the context of my instinctual dis-
equilibrium in dealing with the trauma, when my usual gratifications

have been threatened and disrupted because of my wife's cancer. The snake is furtherfore the very symbol of healing among the ancient Greeks. Aescalepius, the God of Medicine, carries a snake wound around his staff. There is a dedicatory relief from Oropos, circa 400 B.C., showing a healing dream in which the dreamer is touched at the place of illness by the snake, while in the foreground he is depicted healed.

The snake is not only the epiphany of the healing God, but is a symbol of fertility, renewal, life revitalized.

The snake as a symbol of rebirth following death is an ancient, yet ever-present conception which can be traced through sculpture, painting, verse, and the myths of gods, demi-gods, or heroic mortals. This is so because during its yearly hibernation the snake sheds its skin and reappears as if renewed. The wisdom of the serpent, which is suggested by its watchful lidless eye, lies essentially in mankind's having projected into the snake his own secret wish to obtain from the earth a knowledge he cannot find in waking consciousness alone. This is the knowledge of death and rebirth forever withheld except at those times when some transcendent principle, emerging from the depths, makes it available to consciousness. (Henderson, 1963, p. 36)

The snake thus implies a realm of potential Being and the possibility of transformation. The snake is also strongly associated in ancient Greece with the feminine principle, *anima*.

The snake as archetypal expression in my dream—the snake which I fear and loathe during waking—thus points not only to trust that my wife's cancer will be healed (in the face of my waking despair) but also points to what is needed for my own transformation. My conscious side is excessively professorial, and so I am out of balance. The unconscious compensates for this waking rationality by the irruption from the irrational unconscious, in the guise of the snake starting up out of the ground. It is my *anima* that irrupts.

My task becomes even clearer on this archetypal interpretation of my dream. My current feelings belong not only to the event of my wife's cancer, but relate to long-standing issues in my life. I am not only out of balance in virtue of my despair, but also in virtue of my rationality, my excessive critical faculty, my enthrallment to the masculine archetype, Lawgiver, defender of the *Logos*.[13] The task facing me, then, is to develop my irrational side, my receptive *anima*. Until I commit myself to mystery, I am in conflict with my wife, and risk vitiating her struggle against the cancer. So the snake archetype springs up from the collective unconscious at the very moment of my existential crisis and poses a challenge and a choice to excessively rational me, to become a more balanced human being.

5.8 POST-FACE

I wish I could say in retrospect that this dream radically changed my life, that I faced things with confidence and courage and balance ever after on understanding my dream in a Jungian way. The fact is that I sometimes get into worrying and pessimism, as I tend to, and my wife's potential cancer recurrence is available to amply satisfy my actions of worrying and being pessimistic. I remain overly-fond of reason, I confess, frequently calculate the medical probability of her cure, at times pull back from intimacy with her out of fear of loss, and easily lose touch with the mystery surrounding us. It still seems like me!

However, although not curative, the dream has been very helpful to me. I consult the dream when I detect that I am out of balance. I use it as a potent symbol. It shows me a possible way that I habitually tend to neglect, and thereby restores to me my full possibility. Consulted as a creative oracle—as the speaking of Spirit—my dream has healing power.

What is healed is, of course, the person who dreams, not the situation. The dreamer awakened is restored to wholeness in his or her approach to the situation, whatever that situation might be. The dream does not magically predict future states of affairs, I think. Betty Smith (personal communication) puts it beautifully.

For my own part I should say in regard to the prospective aspect of a dream such as this that the serpent image holds great promise, affirms the future in a positive manner but from an impersonal point of view. It must not be read to guarantee the ego's wishes. One can only take a trusting but open attitude; and trust, if it has any ground at all, surely brings up the gods, or else God . . .

Chapter Six

Dreaming Dasein

> *In general terms every* mythos *involves a latent* logos *which demands to be exhibited. That is why there are no symbols without the beginning of interpretation: where one man dreams, prophesies, or poeticizes, another rises up to interpret.*
> Paul Ricoeur, Freud and philosophy: An essay on interpretation. *(1970, p. 19)*

6.1 INTRODUCTION

It is the same old me waking and dreaming. Oh, I sure do some different things in my dream life, things I would have "never dreamt of doing" in my waking life! I can assure you that with my anxieties, you would never catch me swimming all by myself into an ocean grotto, as in the dream of chapter three. In waking, I would have peopled the grotto with octopi and never set foot in the water. Yet it surely felt like me boldly swimming there in my dream.

Now, there is occasionally a bold "side" of me that I value, and this side can come out while dreaming. It happened in this dream that my bold side was to swim boldly, i.e. swim within the horizon of meanings that I project when being bold. So even though I am doing something uncharacteristic of me in my dream-life, it is nonetheless *a way I can be.* There is always my own Being, both dreaming and waking. The question of Being thus arises with respect to the dream life, just as it does with regard to the wake life.

"Da-sein" is Heidegger's term for the being (entity) for whom its own Being (to be) is at issue. Heidegger has provided a profound account of waking Dasein. The aim here is to consider dreaming Dasein.

I do so through the work of the Swiss psychiatrist and Daseinsanalyst, Medard Boss.[1] In this country Boss's work on dreaming has not been influential. In addition to his distancing critique of Freud and Jung, and his depreciation[2] of Rollo May's Americanized existentialism, Boss is estranged from contemporary American psychiatry. Psychiatry is highly science-minded. Boss just waves his hands at all that science.

> The findings from sleep research are certainly highly interesting in their way, and even necessary. But they tell us almost nothing about what they are supposed to represent. Not one of them brings us a single step nearer to an explanation of dreaming as a unique mode of human existence. (Boss, 1977a, p. 10)

This is pretty strong stuff, from the mainstream American psychiatric point of view. Nor could anyone be further than Boss from the computational theory of mind that is the mainstream of cognitive science. Boss is for sure no high-tech "Turing's man"! Finally, as if all this were not enough going against him, Boss frequently "waxes polemical" (i.e. says exactly what he thinks) in a way which is antithetical to American manners. So Boss has not "connected" very well to us, and his contributions accordingly are not appreciated.

The reception to Boss has been further colored by his deep commitment to Heidegger. The Continental tradition in philosophy has been slow to mature in this country, and accordingly Heidegger's work is not widely known.[3] But it is not just the slow American reception of Continental thought that has affected appreciation of Heidegger. Heidegger himself is no help, for a number of reasons.

First of all, Heidegger is hard to "get into," to have the vaguest idea of what he is talking about. As Heidegger became freer of Husserl after his *Being and time* period, he preferred allusiveness to precise formulation in his writing, so the obscurity gets worse as time goes on.[4] Comay calls his style "involuted, aphoristic, disjunctive . . . tortured, tortuous nuggets, resisting the transparent linearity of ordinary language."

A second reason that Heidegger is a millstone around Boss's neck is that Heidegger is anything but "objective" in his approach, in the way scientists understand objectivity. The immediate object of science is the world in which pointers point, Geiger counters count, cloud trails trail, and Hubel-Wiesel detectors detect. Heidegger begins *prior* to that world, in a way reminiscent of Kant's categories of the understanding. We always already find ourselves thrown into a life-world before any positive science might begin. The scientist following his or her world line is also "thrown," thrown into a scientific life-world, a world in which scientific Dasein encounters Geiger counters and the whole caboodle of scientific "ready to hand" tools. Heidegger, as in Husserl before him, wants to get a priori to all this, get to Consciousness, to Being, to *Dasein*. Truly basic inquiry, Heidegger holds, is directed towards the human condition as lived. So the scientific inquiry directed towards world objects is antithetical to Heidegger's basic inquiry into Being.

Heidegger's story, given this orientation, seems unfathomable to the science-minded American mainstream. Heidegger thinks reality is veiled, hidden. (Again there are Kantian overtones of the *ding an sich*.) Our Being unveils the real world. We are an openness, a clearing, where the world appears. We are "ek-static," Heidegger says, we "ek-sist," always already *outside ourselves*, encountering a world. Although our state is outside ourself, our openness is less than the full range of our possibilities. We are situated in certain ways, within a certain horizon that Being generates, within a context that is a "world" of meanings. (It is confusing that Heidegger uses "world" in a number of different ways. The "world" of Being-in-the-world, which is the case of our Being, is the "world" of meanings, not the extant world in which we find ourselves thrown.) Our way of openness specifies past, present, future, now, near and far. The world in which we find ourselves thrown is a function of how we are open to the veiled, how we are "situated.". Our peculiar constrained openness Heidegger calls *Da*—our way of being "there," our presence—and so we are *Daseins*, the beings whose Being is to be situated openness. Heidegger's story thus wanders off in a direction vastly different from positive science.

A third problem that Boss's allegiance to Heidegger brings is that Heidegger's reputation is tainted by his brief flirtation with Nazism and his German nationalism. Consider the entry for Heidegger in *The Encyclopedia of Philosophy*.

> In 1933 Heidegger became the first National Socialist rector of the University of Freiburg, and in a public lecture, "Role of the University in the New Reich," celebrated the advent of a new and glorious Germany . . . a strand of extreme nationalism certainly runs through his work. Holding as he does a mystical view of language, he subscribes with zeal to the widespread opinion that philosophizing is possible, if not only in German, then only in German and Greek. (Grene, 1967, p. 459)

With friends like Heidegger, Boss needs no further enemies! (For a more balanced view of Heidegger, see Hannah Arendt's "Heidegger at Eighty".) In any case, I shall approach dreaming Dasein through Boss in what follows. I begin with a comparison of Boss and Freud, then discuss Boss's dream hermeneutics, and finally consider the origins of the dreaming life-world.

6.2 Boss and Freud

We saw that Edelson and Foulkes (1978) remain basically true to Freud's thought in discussing Freud's dream theory in terms of Chomsky and cognitive science. Freud after all is a progenitor of the computational theory of mind, as can be seen in Peterfreund's information-processing version of psychoanalysis and in Erdelyi. In discussing dreaming from the standpoint of existential phenomenology, however, there is a sharp break with the Freudian tradition. Boss acknowledges some debt, but nevertheless has basic disagreements with his predecessors.

> Naturally, it should not be forgotten that no new dream theory could ever have seen the light of day had it not been preceded by the decisive, concrete observations of Freud, Adler and Jung.

Yet the dream theories of these pioneers lead us astray from the outset . . . (1977a, p. 7)

Let us consider the gulf between Boss and Freud.

Now, Freud was your real science type. He had done significant bench research in brain science and psychopharmacology before he founded psychoanalysis. There is a certain irony to Freud's deep commitment to science, since Freud's subject matter—psychiatric patients no less—is difficult to do hard science with. Freud strove very hard to be scientifically objective but his field of inquiry just was "soft." Freud (1895) had hoped to maintain links to objective neuroscience, but eventually decided not to wait for neuroscience to catch up; he would just forge ahead with psychology, but in a thoroughly objective manner. So Freud's predilections remained staunchly scientific, despite the softness of psychoanalytic subject matter.

Freud's scientific attitude was greatly influenced by Helmholtz, who was a dominant figure in the German universities in the late nineteenth century. (Helmholtz is indeed the founding father of the computational theory of mind; his "unconscious inferences" according to which perceptions are produced are just the computations of logical brain systems.)[5] Helmholtz's fundamental work in thermodynamics on the conservation of energy sets the tone for Freud's discussion of psychic energies, the so-called "economic" point of view, which was crucial to Freud's dream theory.[6] Helmholtz wanted to get behind visible effects to their underlying physical causes; he reduced the given to more basic forces. Freud similarly longed to get to the more fundamental, to expose the pasteboard mask of surface phenomena (like the manifest dream) and penetrate to the real underlying mechanisms (like unconscious wishful thoughts) that lawfully caused those surface phenomena. Freud, like Helmholtz, wants to reduce what is given to something more fundamental.

Boss is quite the opposite. What is given is sacred. (Recall Husserl's phenomenological clarion call: *To the things themselves!* (It somehow sounds more rousing in German.)) The *phenomenon* given is not to be discarded; it is given by the very Being towards which the Bossian *logos* is directed. The phenomenon given is the only game in town for Boss. He is not interested in causal mechanism, like Freud, but in Being. Boss's concern is with what it is to *be* a human being—with Being-in-the-"world" and our thrownness into the life-world—not with an objective and reductive analysis of the human being. (There are three Heideggerian senses of "being" to keep track of: (1) Being as the to-be, (2) beings as entities, (3) being as meaning.[7]

So there is a wide gulf between Boss and Freud. Boss's great contribution, I think, is to pick up dreaming in the Continental ontological fashion, to inquire into dreaming Being, counterpoint to Edelson and the early Foulkes' development of Freudian dream theory in the Anglo-American spirit of linguistic analysis. The next section discusses Boss's clinical use of dreaming.

6.3 THE HERMENEUTICS OF DREAMING BEING

Boss insists that he does not "interpret" dreams, like the Freudians, Jungians, Szondians, American existentialists, and whoever. Some Heideggerians "encountering" his "Dreaming and the dreamed in the Daseinsanalytical way of seeing,"[8] however, see Boss as arbitrarily interpreting dreams, and no better in principle than the people Boss so vigorously criticizes.[9] A discussion of this tension will illuminate Bossian hermeneutics.

Gendlin says that "many different interpretations of the same dream, using the same concepts of 'bearing' [comportment] and 'possibility' can be made with any one dream."[10] There is, of course, *some* characteristic bearing and *some* possibility.

> But from hearing a given dream, or from observing the person in waking life, different interpreters will arrive at different conclusions. They will choose different dimensions to look at, and they may also disagree about the person on a given dimension. (Gendlin, 1977, p. 60)

Gendlin finds that in Boss "dream interpretations are free floating,"[11] and "seemingly quite arbitrary."[12]

The general direction of looking (how one bears oneself in life, or could bear oneself) is excellent and valuable. But no methodological criteria are offered for establishing this or that interpretation as the appropriate one. Boss's personal preoccupations and values seem to be the guide. (Gendlin, 1977, p. 64)

But I think that Gendlin does not distinguish sharply enough what Boss means by "interpretation."

What Boss is objecting to in Freud is *translational interpretation*, in which our thrownness "in" the life-world is transposed into something else. In the case of dreams Freudian translational interpretation is easily seen. Freud himself compared the dream to a rebus: dream *pictures* are to be translated into underlying, more fundamental, dream *thoughts*.

What Boss wants to focus on is Being while dreaming, instead of translating into something else hidden. Boss focuses on dreaming Being-in-the-"world". His interpretation is not of the dream but of the person's unique Being-in-the-"world" while dreaming. There is plenty of room for conflicting interpretations of a person's Being-in-the-"world", heaven knows.

Bossian interpretation is thus directed towards opening up Dasein's possibilities by indicating the person's horizon, what "world" lies hidden to the person, by specifying comportments. As Ricoeur says of understanding texts in general,

Understanding is not addressed therefore to grasping a fact but to the apprehension of a possibility and our utmost potentialities. . . . to understand a text, we shall say, is not to find an inert meaning which is contained therein, rather it is to unfold the possibility of being which is indicated by the text. (Ricoeur, 1978, p. 153)

Bossian interpretation unfolds possibilities of Being indicated by the dream text. The value of discussing dream Being, Boss points out in a discussion of one of Freud's patients, is that completely different relations become apparent in the dreaming situation. Through waking reflection on the dream and discussion of the dream comportments, a person can become aware of possibilities for existing, aware of possible ways of comportment:

> ... it very often occurs that significances which were previously unknown approach and dawn for a person *for the first time* in his life while dreaming. (Boss, 1977b, p. 32)

One reason dreams may have a "decisive therapeutic impact," Boss says, is that significances are "sensibly perceptibly" given, and as such they can more easily be dealt with.

> ... these significances, previously not admitted, often address a person during dreaming only in foreign, sensibly perceptible present givens. . . . In their solid, sensibly perceptible presence, they signal to him, so to speak, with a large red flag. (Boss, 1977b, p. 32)

What is dreamed, then, can draw the attention of the waking person to

> specific, existential, non-objectifiable possibilities of relating which had previously remained concealed both in dreaming and in being awake. This occurrence can clarify for the reawakened person his relations to himself and to his environment and shared world. (Boss, 1977b, p. 32)

Dreams are thus therapeutically powerful stuff for Boss.

But how is the interpretation of dreaming Being—not translation of the manifest dream—to be validated? Gendlin brings this out beautifully. With a "good" interpretation a phenomenon shows itself, viz. some further aspect of the dream fits or stands out. Something new is "lifted up by the interpretation," "what *was implicit* suddenly stands out."[13] The good interpretation picks up a thread; it leads further, and not in a mechanically logical way. Moreover, the good interpretation

> makes sense not only conceptually but in reference to something directly experienced as well, something now lifted out which can talk back, which can show itself as other and more than the words which lifted it out. (Gendlin, 1977, p. 67)

The phenomenon lifted out by a good interpretation is "always more and different than the very statement which helped to lift it out."[14] A flowing dialectic ensues.

But it is apparent that non-existential interpretations can also be "good" in Gendlin's sense, to the extent that they bear upon a person's Being-in-the-"world." So Gendlin's cogent criterion for interpretation doesn't really help in adjudicating between interpretations from different schools. Surely what Freud means by unconscious wishes has important influence on a person's Being-in-the-"world," and so dream interpretation along these traditional psychoanalytic lines will open up Dasein's possibilities, just as would supposedly direct Daseinsanalytic comments. Boss's interpretations of dreaming Being are very powerful, as he illustrates them (and to my mind more appreciative of the human condition than Freud). But I think that is mainly a function of Boss's clinical charisma rather than any allegiance to Daseinsanalytic principles. After all, nearly all species of psychotherapy and sound clinicans of most persuasions turn dreams to good therapeutic use.

Having given some general sense of where Boss takes the discussion of dreaming within his Heideggerian frame, we can turn to the specific issue of the present inquiry. Where does the life-world of dreaming come from according to Boss? How is it that dreaming Dasein finds himself or herself thrown *kerplunk* in a world?

6.4 UNITARY DASEIN

Boss emphasizes that Dasein is a unitary being.

At one time, a person exists as a dreaming being (Wesen); at other times, as a waking being. (Boss, 1977b, p. 8)

Dreaming and waking are equally primitive and essential *ways of being,* possible ways of existing. Out of this parity, "when dreaming we usually fancy ourselves to be fully awake."[15]

The issue more fundamental than dreaming and waking is that of Being, or existence.

> This existing of ours, whether it occurs in a waking or a dreaming way, immediately presents itself to be known as a primordial Being-in-the-world. (Boss, 1977b, p. 8)

And we are always in the condition of thrownness.

> There never was, and there never will be, a person who, were he to reflect upon his own Dasein, would not find it from the outset to be thrown into a world. (Boss, 1977b, p. 8)

We are thrown into the dream world just as we are thrown into the awake world, i.e. our dreaming and waking thrownness are indiscernable. Whether dreaming or waking,

> Whenever we pay careful attention to the way in which we, as existing persons, are "in" the world, we always find ourselves already, and from the outset, to be beings to whom the most various things and creatures speak from out of the openness of a world-domain. (Boss, 1977b, p. 8)

The various things and creatures disclosed to us always already are significant to us in accordance with our situatedness and purposes, our horizon. At the same time

> we also always see ourselves already answering—acting and thinking in response with the perceived address of what is encountered. (Boss, 1977b, p. 8)

We have the ability to be addressed by encountered things and creatures, and also the ability to answer. For Boss we Daseins *are* nothing other than *possibilities for receptive and responsive, alert world-disclosiveness.*[16]

Although Boss emphasizes that Being-in-the-"world" equally characterizes both ways of existence, he picks up on what we called in chapter two, following Rechtschaffen, the "single-mindedness" of dreams. He emphasizes that we are less open in dreaming than waking, have less breadth and freedom, are less developed and mature. There is an "existential constriction" during dreaming.

Our awakening (Er-wachen) and only our awakening thus leads us out into the full development of our being (Wesen). It leads us up out of the less free dimensions of dreaming Being-in-the-world and up to the greatest possible freedom of our existence as fully awake, to the attainment of the actual meaning and purpose of our Dasein. (Boss, 1977b, p. 31).

As a good Heideggerian, Boss does not value dreaming as much as waking, for only while waking can Dasein hope to achieve its full possibilities for Being-in-the-"world." In any case, whatever the supposed limitations of dreaming Dasein, Dasein is unitary for Boss across dreaming and waking, entirely consistent with the argument of chapter two that dreaming and waking life-worlds are indiscernable. But Boss differs sharply from chapter one with respect to production of the dream world and our life in it, as we next see.

6.5 DASEIN AND THE DREAMING LIFE-WORLD

Dreaming Dasein for Boss is essentially uncreative. Dasein does not create the dream world but is given it by Being, just like the wake world is given. Dasein has *no responsibility* for the dream world; Dasein does not formatively create the dream as I argued in chapter one.

No one, least of all the dreamer herself, would have needed to *make* the givens of her dream-world—nor *could* she have accomplished such a creating. That which she perceived while dreaming was already there from the outset, when she began to know something of herself while dreaming—precisely as is the case of the givens of her being awake. In both states of our existing we are always and from the onset "thrown" into the relationship of the "givens" of our world. (Boss, 1977b, p. 21)

It is indeed striking that for an existentialist, to whom responsibility is central, we are not responsible for the dream world. Even the title of Boss's book (1977a) *in the original German* shows Dasein's lack of responsibility for the life-world of dreams. The English title is "I dreamt last night" but the German title is *Es traumte mir vergangene Nacht,* literally "it dreamt to me last night.")

> ... it is not I who produce something out of myself and give it forth when I dream, but rather that something is given and sent *to me* (dative); I have only to answer accordingly in thought and action. (Boss, 1977b, p. 34)

This can be illustrated more closely by one of Boss's dream discussions.[17]

A patient dreams seeing her analyst with an "unkempt, wild growth of beard," when in her waking life he has always been clean-shaven. The dream experience is not at all one of an *image* of a beard, Boss observes, "but as being a real beard made of the stuff actual beards are made of." However, there is no evidence to indicate, he thinks, that the beard is produced by the dreamer. If we stick with the dream phenomenon, what we find is,

> As far as the dreamer's perception is concerned, all that really happens is that a decidedly bearded analyst manifests himself in the light of her dreaming existence. (Boss, 1977a, p. 65)

The bearded analyst is given for Boss just like the clean-shaven analyst of waking life, and Dasein just lives in relation to it.

But the veiled world of waking is *autonomous* of Dasein, abides and awaits unveiling by Dasein. The dream world, in contrast, is given by Being.

> That which gives, which sends the givens of my dream-worlds to shine forth and thus to be in the understanding openness of my existence—i.e. the "Es" in "Es traumte mir . . . "—is the event of Being as such . . . (Boss, 1977b, p. 34)

Being emits the dream-world. The Being as such that gives the dream world is primordial, a priori to space and time, and a priori to all beings encountered. To be humanly dreaming is to be given dream-worlds.

If we persist in inquiring as to *how* Being manages to give dreaming Dasein the dream world (since it is not already there for the unveiling, as in waking), we run into Boss's disdain of mechanism and a typical Heideggerian fog. There is a dynamic tension in Heidegger between the openness, the disclosedness, of Being, and the hiddenness of Being. "Openness and hiddenness are . . . mutual determinants of each other."[18] That which is hidden in Being can be disclosed to Being.

This Being as such can bring forth and release from itself into its unhidden presence that which is given to the dreaming person. (Boss, 1977b, p. 34)

The phrasing of such Heideggerian claims about dream appearances is notably cumbersome.

. . . Being as such—this "Es"—is the "whence" out of whose hiddenness everything which is comes to appearance by coming into the unhiddenness of its presence. This presencing embraces everything human, including man's dream-phenomena. (Boss, 1977b, p. 34)

But at bottom Boss's explanation of the dream world is to point at Being and say baldly, "*He's* the culprit." Boss is content with an account of Being in which the dream world moves from hiddenness to openness because that's just the way Being is, giving to Dasein the dream world which Dasein answers in thought and action. The dream world comes to Dasein just because *es gibt.*

To sustain this *es gibt* posture, it is necessary to restrict one's observations entirely to the dream phenomenon and avoid free association to the dream like the plague, for otherwise the relation to waking becomes compelling. This restriction is easy enough for Boss to do, since phenomenology assiduously attends "to the things themselves," not what they make us think of.[19] But as soon as we reflect on the dream we are reminded of waking events. Reflecting at the time of waking from my dream of swimming into the grotto (chapter three), I was immediately reminded of having imagined the half-dome over the swimming pool the preceding day. On waking reflectively from my dream of operating the medical equipment (chapter one), I just remembered (*es gibt*) trying to find the box of Kleenex when I had awakened sneezing earlier that night. Although surely my associations to my dream are guided by my own theoretical predilections, and the patient's associations pick up on the therapist's theoretical persuasion, dreams do have compelling connections (a "family resemblance" as discussed in 1.7) to waking episodes, especially recent ones. The dreaming life-world thus has *something* to do with past waking life-worlds. We cannot just stick our head in the sand and pronounce *es gibt*.

The lengths Boss has to go in avoiding the relevance of free-association is shown in another dream discussion.[20] A patient dreams of being with her (actually healthy) friend who has a serious heart disease. As she slowly awakened, "she came to realize ever more succinctly that she herself and not her friend was suffering terribly from a 'heartsickness'," viz. her unrequited love for her analyst. The patient had been completely oblivious of her emotional frustration while dreaming, even though while waking it had been "present to a certain degree," Boss says.

Now surely the waking feelings and meanings of heartsickness, partially owned and partially obscured, had something to do with the dream. Are we to think it just happens that *es gibt* a dreaming life-world uncannily relevant to waking, and in a "sensually perceptible, temporally present" way?[21] Apparently so.

> Nothing whatsoever justifies the assumption that her emotional 'heartsickness' nevertheless did continue to be there in her dreaming state as 'psychic being' but was only temporarily 'symbolically' hidden behind the 'dream image' of a diseased bodily organ. (Boss, 1977a, p. 202)

But the plain fact recounted by Boss is that the dream immediately reminded the patient of her waking heartsickness, and in an emotionally impactive way so that she became fully aware of it (consistent with Gendlin's criterion for validity).

So the *connection* between the patient's waking heartsickness and the dreamed friend's heart disease is an indubitable fact of waking reflection on the dream. That *es gibt* the dream world must have *something* to do with waking. Either *es gibt* the dream world by compositing mnemic copies of waking Dasein or *es gibt* the dream world by creating it *de novo* from past meanings.

This result fractures for Boss the unity of Dasein across dreaming and waking; in waking the veiled world awaits unveiling by human Being, whereas in dreaming an upsurge of Being creates an unveiled world. The only way to repair the unity of Dasein, demanded by the essential indiscernability of dreaming and waking and also suggested by the clinical value of interpretation of Being via dream Being, is to say that waking Being also creates the world *de novo*, as was said in chapter three. But this outcome would start Boss (and Heidegger) down the slippery slope from the staunch direct realism of the existential tradition to a monadological realism. (It is often thought that the tradition holds a transcendental idealism, not a direct realism. Although there are certainly idealistic tendencies, especially in Husserl, I think the basic thrust is realistic.)

6.6 MONADIC DASEIN

My meditations on dreaming keep leading to this weird monadology, this isolated "bubble of perception," as the sorcerer says, in which the dream world is constituted *de novo* by dreaming thought, like Athena from Zeus' brow. Out of the critique of the current theories of dream world formation, out of the essential indiscernability of dreaming and waking life-worlds, and out of deep respect for what is parsimonious and what is plausible with respect to biological evolution, the extremely uncommonsensical conclusion has issued that in waking life, too, we are monads, thinking the very perceptible world in which we find ourselves thrown.

My proposal is that the monadic organism's to-be—the human monad's existing—is at heart a creative movement. This creative movement is the same across dreaming and waking phases. Monadic existing has two moments. First, it spontaneously generates encodings of possible life-worlds that function as a horizon, i.e. as abstract specifications at the monad's various interfaces with the surrounding energy sea. A peculiar mechanism in relation to the surround then comes into play.

In the case of waking, where the information of the flowing array of stimulus energies passes freely across the monad's sensory receptors, certain abstract specifications (tunings) of the neural filters are contingently matched by the input flux. All the monad can ever know is the extent to which its abstract specs have been met; it is "methodologically solipsistic" in Fodor's sense.[22] Those specifications matched are enabled to form an actual life world. Unmatched specifications remain purely cognitive.

In the case of dreaming, previous abstract specifications (typically from the preceding day, but also from childhood) become reoperative. The specifications thus reoperative in dreaming are picked out not by any match with the input flux, which is after all cutoff during sleep, but by our wishes, especially highly single-minded wishes we are not conscious of during waking. (That is, we are not aware of, indeed resist awareness of, making certain specifications.) Those specifications amplified by wish, reoperative while dreaming, formatively create concrete life-worlds. In some dreams, especially when existential crisis opens us up, archetypal specifications become strongly operative.

A monad thus creative is truly both a clearing and a constrained openness. This monad is a clearing in virtue of supporting production of a specific life-world out of the possible life-worlds; the monad clears up the confusion of possibilia in "enpresenting" an actual world. The monad is a "constrained" openness in terms of what it brings to the match; it is open to the match, but in a certain way, in accordance with a certain horizon.

Again, note this critical difference betweeen the present monadology and Heidegger. The monad's creative principle does not include any *ekstatic* component which puts the monad (and Dasein for that matter) in the paradoxical position of being always already outside itself, God knows how.[23] "Ekstasis" is replaced by "formativity" in the present monadological account, and that is a fundamental shift.

On the monadological view, dreaming Dasein gives a perspicuous rendition of Being. (Curiously, Boss does not think of dreaming Dasein as *via regia* to Being. He retains the bias of academic western philosophy against dreams; he says dreams are existentially "constricted.") For the present view, *the monadic essence is producing/product.* (This "producing/

product" in the monadic account plays the role of act/object in the intentional account of direct realism, but without the ontological gap between immanent act and transcendent object that is so vexing in the latter.)

Our "thrownness" in the world, then, is just that of the producer in relation to his or her product; a continuous producing together with a product continuously produced is our monadic way of existing. Of course we "fall" inauthentically into commerce with the product, and "forget" that our monadic Being is producing/product. But dreaming brings us up short; when we bracket the natural attitude in the dream *epoche*, then we can come to appreciate our essential creativity while dreaming. Indeed, showing that the dream life is our own formative creation has been a central goal of this book. Our *logos* through dreaming points to producing/product, and then our waking Being is appreciated. An isolated bubble of creativity nested within an ambient energy sea . . .

6.7 PRODUCING/PRODUCT AND *MĀYĀ*

Ontologically speaking, the present account takes a significant departure from Heidegger, *viz.* the life-world is created *de novo* by us rather than having its own being which awaits our ekstases.My account is much closer ontologically to ancient Indian philosophy, to the doctrine of māyā. (My appreciation of this connection was greatly enhanced by a late reading of Wendy Doniger O'Flaherty's *Dreams, Illusion and other Realities*, which concentrates especially on the *Yogavāsistha* (c. 600-1200 A.D.).)

One meaning of *māyā* is translated as "illusion" but it also has a basis in the verbal root *mā* which means "to make." Thus O'Flaherty calls *māyā* "creative power,"[24] "artistic creation,"[25] "the process of creation."[26] She quotes Gonda on *māyā* in terms of "converting an idea into dimensional reality,"[27] which is just what I have called "formative creativity." Indeed, O'Flaherty speaks of the sage Vasistha as entering "the dreaming sleep in which we create, as the gods create, by emitting images."[28] The two meanings of *māyā*—making and illusion—are reformulated here as producing/product. In O'Flaherty's hands, we come to understand *māyā* through discussion of ancient "myths" about dreaming. The present investigation of twentieth-century approaches to dreaming has led to the concept of producing/product that converges on the concept of *māyā*.

Although the convergence is striking, there remain some differences between the ontology discussed by O'Flaherty and the present ontology; these differences have to do with mechanism. Indian philosophy had its Demiurge, the divine craftsman.

> The image of the creator as an artisan can be traced back to the Rg Vedic hymns to Viśvakarman, the All-Maker, who is imagined as a sculptor, a smith, a woodcutter, or a carpenter. . . . This is an underlying assumption of the *Yogavāsistha;* God is the artist who paints the pictures that we mistake for the world. (O'Flaherty, 1984, p. 293)

So the mechanism of *māyā* entails a God operating the machine. For the present account, in contrast, the mechanism is monadic, a possible worlds machine, that generates an a priori set of possibilities through general mechanisms (genetic prescription + random variation), a set modified by experience, and creates by selection from this plenum of possibilia. (See 4.5) No external divine force is required to energize creation. However, the image of the All-Maker as artisan should not be taken too literally; there are deeper currents to Hindu philosophy.

Now *māyā* is the "art" of the God *Rudra,* who sketches images in our dreaming minds.[29]

> For Rudra to think of something is for him both to make it exist and to find that it has always existed as part of him. These two kinds of creation—making and finding—are the same . . . (O'Flaherty, 1984, p. 212)

O'Flaherty thinks making and finding are the same because

> . . . in both cases the mind—or the Godhead—imposes its idea on the spirit/matter dough of reality, cutting it up as with a cookie-cutter, now into stars, now into hearts, now into elephants, now into swans. It makes them, and it finds them already there, like a *bricoleur,* who makes new forms out of *objet trouvès* [found objects]. (O'Flaherty, 1984, p. 212, brackets added)

This conception of Rudra is reminiscent of the syntactically creative *bricoleur* who composits Freud's dream world out of found memory traces. (See 1.2b) But Rudra could also be read as formatively creative.

> Rudra's mind is the mold that stamps out the images, all of which derive from him. He stamps this mold on the spirit/matter continuum of the universe in such a way that it breaks up into the separate (or, rather, apparently separate) consciousnesses of all of us. The images that he sketches in our minds were already there—in the continuum, and in our minds; but we cannot know them until his mind touches ours, until he "joins his mind to [our] mind." (O'Flaherty, 1984, p. 212)

Here the images could be considered to be "already there" *implicately,* enfolded to the continuum, and the joining of Rudra's mind to ours unfolds the images.

So in giving Rudra a monadic possible worlds reading, making and finding are exactly the same, viz. a selecting from the a priori plenum of possibilia. Although the continuum—the spirit/matter dough of reality—appears undifferentiated (a chaos of vibratory interference), possibilities are enfolded to it, unfolding to Rudra's touch, like Bohm's holomovement unfolds explicate existentia from the implicate order. The world of both dreaming and waking is *māyā*-product, made by a Leibnizian machine operation.

6.8 SUMMARY

Boss discusses dreaming in the context of Heideggerian existential phenomenology. Waking reflection on dreaming allows an interpretation in existential terms of a person's way of Being-in-the-"world" (a person's horizon of meanings) as alternative to the Freudian terms of an unconscious mind. Boss thus connects up dreaming to the ontological concerns of the Continental philosophical tradition. Boss gives no account of how the dreaming life-world is created, but it is clear that the dreamer is not responsible. Being just gives the dream. *Es traumte mir . . .* Being dreams to me . . . Boss doesn't think that any account is needed, however, since Being is foundational to any causal mechanism that might be discussed. But in waking reflection on the dream, free associations connect the dream to waking life (especially "residues" of the preceding day) in a compelling fashion, even though Boss would eschew free associations out of devotion to the dream phenomena as given and fear of contaminating Being by theory. Once the connection between dreaming and waking is acknowledged, however, then to save the unity of Dasein across dreaming and waking, Being must "give," i.e. create, the wake world too, rather than "give," i.e. unveil, an autonomous wake world. *The monadic Dasein's essential creative movement*—Being's Temporality, *māyā* as making-finding—*is producing/product.*

Epilogue

The twentieth century has witnessed great progress in our understanding of and involvement with dreaming. This began spec-
tacularly in 1900 with the publication of Freud's *The Interpretation of
Dreams*. (The book was actually ready in late 1899, but the publisher
chose the more portentous year for the title page.) Chapter One of *The
Interpretation of Dreams* shows the sorry state of dream theory before
Freud. Dreams were just meaningless and mechanical biological processes for the *fin d'siecle* community of scholars. By the time we finish
chapter seven, dreams are meaningful expressions of an unconscious
mind, and on interpretation according to Freudian hermeneutics provide a *via regia* to the unconscious mind. Since the unconscious mind is
also expressed in the psychopathology of the patients that consulted
Freud, the dream was further linked to psychiatric theory and praxis,
and through that domain, to human nature and culture at large. Freud's
achievement was thus monumental, although that is difficult to see in a

contemporary frame, so familiar are we with the profound significance of dreaming.

Jung added crucial dimensions, I think. Jung was able to glimpse the deep *a priori* in dreams; dreams can sometimes express the "archetypal" predispositions given by the genome. Jung also saw far better than Freud the healthy side of things, our natural vitality when left unimpeded. Dreams are *healing*, if we understand and use them rightly. So far was Jung from Freud in this regard that he thought the unconscious mind archaically wise! Thus although Jung built on Freud, he brought a vastly different world view to dreams, the view of the mystic and the *philosophia perennis*. Jung saw clearly the mysterious, "numinous," spiritual, trans-personal dimension of dreams.

Boss adds an existential correction of Freud. Although Boss sees himself as providing a radical critique of Freud within a Heideggerian frame, I see him as providing an important humanizing influence. In Boss the emphasis shifts from unconscious thoughts underlying dreaming to Dasein's Being as a unitary existing with respect to which dreaming and waking are equal and originary *ways* of existing.

A biological correction of Freud was initiated by Aserinsky, Dement and Kleitman's discovery of the association between REM sleep and dreaming. (Not that Freud lacked a biological dimension, but the biology available to him was primitive.) A cognitive dimension was added to Freud by Edelson and Foulkes. (Not that Freud lacked a cognitive dimension, but there was no cognitive science in his day.) So the understanding and use of dreams launched by Freud in 1900 was subsequently corrected and advanced biologically, cognitively, existentially and transpersonally (which pretty much covers the waterfront).

Recent discussions of lucid dreaming, notably by Castaneda and LaBerge, bring something new. Now dreaming becomes a basis for appreciating our enormous creativity, for understanding the fuller possibilities of human awareness, and a praxis for actually achieving those possibilities. In Castaneda, lucid dreaming becomes the way to freedom, to "the fire from within."[1]

My basic endeavor here has been to use dreaming for philosophical purposes, and at the same time maintain psychoanalytic, biological, cognitive, existential and transpersonal understandings. A strategic existential shift in attention with respect to Freud is from interpretation of the hidden underlying meaning of manifest dreams to dream Being as a mode of existence, i.e. from "the hermeneutics of suspicion,"[2] as Ricoeur says, to ontology. I have tried to show that dreams investigated in this way lead to a peculiar "monadological realism," according to which we each are isolated in our own "bubble of perception," dreaming and waking, each constituting our life-world *de novo* in accordance with the affordances of the surrounding energy sea and our own intentions. To the extent that the affordances of our surroundings and the abstract specifications of our intentions are the same, our worlds are coherent. This inter-subjective coherence gives the compelling *illusion* of human closeness, but we are in fact profoundly isolated from one another.

By thus taking dreaming as *via regia* to the human condition, it turns out with everything scary and lonely. We care a lot about our seemingly self-subsistent life-worlds and the people we love, and it is distressing to think that we are each just severed creative "clearings" where a certain show is playing, and we are ultimately responsible for what is going on in the clearing, no less. O'Flaherty provides some reassurance, however, since "*māyā* is disturbing only to those who do not understand it, who are not enlightened."[3] Jung, too, is reassuring, for our deepest intentional specifications are shared by humankind, archetypal predispositions precipitated in common out of evolutionary time. We may in fact be existentially isolated in a "bubble of perception," yet we know that the bubbles of others are similarly "homey," and this dulls the edge of our isolation.[4] Once we choose the existential vortex of the life-world (*saṃsāra*) over release from it (*mokṣa*), the challenge of our world thrownness is to develop the possibilities of our monadic Being, to move towards a living that is sheer Openness. Our palliative is to laugh a lot, Kundera-like, about our ridiculous isolation, our ineluctable situatedness, and the uncontrollable contingencies that the surrounding energy sea affords. Our resource remains the immense creativity of the wake life, unveiled by study of the dream life.

Notes

Chapter One: The Creativity of Dreaming

1. Hobson and McCarley, 1977, p. 1347
2. For a thorough and insightful discussion of Freud's view of consciousness, see Natsoulas, 1984 and 1985.
3. Foulkes, 1985
4. Dement and Kleitman, 1957; Globus, 1970a
5. Hobson and McCarley, 1977; Crick and Mitchison, 1983
6. LaBerge, 1985, ps. 82-87
7. LaBerge, 1985, p. 54, and note 10 on p. 258
8. For a general discussion of Castaneda's sorceric "man of knowledge," see M. Globus and G. Globus, 1983.
9. Edelson, 1973; Foulkes, 1978
10. Boss, 1977b, p. 7
11. Ibid, p. 8
12. Freud, 1900, p. 538
13. Ibid, ps. 543 and 565

14. Ibid, p. 546
15. Ibid, p. 547
16. Ibid, p. 546
17. Ibid, p. 324
18. Ibid, p.106
19. Freud, 1917, p. 113
20. Ibid, p. 114
21. Haugeland, 1982
22. Hobson and McCarley, 1977, p. 1347
23. Ibid, p. 1347
24. Crick and Mitchison, 1983, p. 113
25. For another critique of Edelman, see Mahony and Singh, 1975.
26. Edelson, 1973, p. 273
27. Ibid, p. 273
28. Chomsky is not always consistent in this regard, however. See Dreyfus, 1979, p. 332-335.
29. Chomsky, 1980, p. 222
30. Freud, 1900, p. 293
31. Dreyfus, 1979, p. 120-128
32. Foulkes, 1985, chapter two
33. Globus, Phoebus and Moore, 1970b; Kripke and Sonnenschein, 1978
34. Wilber, 1982, p. 163

Chapter Two: Dream Phenomenology

1. See the presentation of Aristotle's theory by Wijsenbeek-Wijler (1978) and the discussion of both ancient Greek and Indian dream theory by Gupta (1971).
2. Quoted by Malcolm, 1959, p. 102
3. LaBerge, 1985, chapter four
4. Malcolm, 1959, p. 51
5. Ibid, p. 65
6. Ibid, p. 87
7. Ibid, p. 86
8. Against Malcolm's claim that dream reports of a dream life make no sense because they cannot be independently verified, see the articles by Siegler (1977), Chappell (1977) and Dunlop (1977).
9. As was already pointed out by Plato in *The Republic*, " ... the *logos* of a dream is always in some way tied to the waking character of the dreamer." (Alderman, 1977, p. 103)

10. For a more extensive discussion of Dennett's argument, see Globus (1986a). This type of dream is also featured in the *Yogavāsistha* (c. 600-1200 A.D.), as discussed by O'Flaherty (1984, Chapter four).
11. Freud, 1900, p. 496
12. Ibid, p. 498
13. Dennett, 1978, p. 136
14. Heidegger, 1927 (1982)
15. Rechtschaffen, 1978, p. 100
16. Ibid, p. 98
17. Ibid, p. 97
18. Ibid, p. 101
19. Ibid, p. 102
20. Ibid, p. 102
21. Freud, 1900, p. 169
22. Castaneda, 1984
23. Castaneda, 1984, p.176

Chapter Three: Dreaming and Waking

1. Gibson, 1979
2. O'Flaherty, 1984
3. Wijsenbeek-Wijler, 1978
4. Rechtschaffen, 1978; Foulkes, 1985
5. Castaneda, 1973
6. J.J. Gibson is, I believe, the natural scientific ally of these Continental philosophers. Certainly Husserl's *intent* was to be a direct realist. (D.W. Smith, 1982) Although Heidegger's formulation is a highly original one, it remains a version of direct realism. His "ekstases" are supposed to bridge the ontological gap between the immanent mind and the transcendent world.
7. Evans, 1984, p. 141
8. Ibid, p. 155, bracket added
9. Pylyshn, 1984
10. Foulkes, 1985, ps. 71-77
11. Moline, 1981, p. 87
12. This is where the most primitive level of sense data or hyletic data, tied to input through the constancy-hypothesis, enters in for the traditional theory. See Gurwitsch (1964, p. 271) on Husserl in this regard.
13. See Q. Smith's discussion (1977) of hyletic data for Husserl's taxonomy.
14. Sellars, 1963, p. 26

15. Weimer, 1973
16. See the discussions edited by Hooker (1982).
17. Castaneda, 1973
18. Pylyshn, 1984
19. *A course in miracles.* Vol. one. Text. Foundation for inner peace.
20. Ibid, p. 351
21. Ibid, p. 473
22. Ibid, p. 350
23. Ibid, p. 351

Chapter Four: The Cognitive Approach to Dreaming

1. Haugeland, 1985
2. Bolter, 1984
3. Neisser, 1967, p. 146 and p. 285.
4. Kerr et al, 1982
5. Neisser, 1976, p. 31-32 (See also the critique of Neisser by Foulkes, 1978, p. 165-167.)
6. Neisser's schemata play a comparable role in his theory to noesis and noema for Husserl (1913), and to intentional state with its conditions of satisfaction for Searle (1983). See also Mandler (1985) on schemata.
7. Pylyshn, 1981, 1984
8. Neisser, 1967, chapter 6
9. Ibid, p. 281
10. Ibid, p. 95
11. Ibid, p. 97
12. This tendency is by no means confined to Neisserian cognitive psychology. Rock, for example, talks of "literal percepts" which are "in close correspondence with the proximal stimulus." (Rock, 1983, p. 101)
13. Foulkes, 1985, p. 158
14. Ibid, p. 8
15. Ibid, p. 40
16. Foulkes, 1982, p. 185
17. Neisser, 1976, p. 138
18. Ibid, p. 131
19. Foulkes, 1982, p. 165
20. Foulkes, 1978, p. 162
21. van Dam, 1984
22. My discussion primarily follows the work of Jerne. I focus on the B cell whose story is simpler and better known than the T cell. (See Marrack and Kappler (1986) on the T cell.)
23. Leder, 1982; Tonegawa, 1985

24. Newell, 1973; Anderson, 1983; Haugeland, 1985
25. Haugeland, 1985, p. 159
26. I have discussed the brain in optical terms in more detail elsewhere. (Globus, 1981, 1985 and especially 1987) The present account differs in that previously I thought of the "plenum of possibilia" as a central unified "holoworld," enfolding all possible worlds, from which the results of input analysis unfolded actual worlds. But here the "plenum of possibilia" comprises a set of distinct filters on input that are auto-transformed to actual worlds. Both present and previous accounts emphasize the a priori, however. This should be distinguished from a posteriori theories (e.g. by Pribram (1971) and Cavanagh (1975, 1984, 1985)). Cavanagh (1975) traces the original notion of thinking about the brain in wave terms to Lashley (1929). For other important contributions in this area, see Bohm (1980), Pribram, Nuwer and Baron (1974), and Yevick (1975). On optical information processing, see Vander Lugt (1964), Stroke (1969), Stark (1982) and Pepper (1986).
27. Glass, 1984
28. Leger and Lee, 1982.
29. The hyperneuron shifts specifications from *de dicto* to *de re* as a consequence of "imprinting."
30. For example, see the discussion of solving optimization problems utilizing neural networks with effectively symmetric synaptic connections by Hopfield and Tank (1986).

Chapter Five: The Dream as Oracle

1. Stevens, 1983, has greatly illuminated this murky Jungian notion.
2. Stevens, 1983, p. 23
3. Ibid, p. 44
4. Ibid, p. 90
5. Stevens (1983, p. 43) makes a Jungian connection to Chomsky, comparing the archetypes to the a priori universal grammar that generates surface speech, counterpoint to the Freudian connection to Chomsky discussed in 1.4.
6. Foulkes, 1985
7. Ibid, p. 192
8. Ibid, p. 194
9. Ibid, p. 204
10. Ibid, p. 204
11. Jung, 1960
12. Castaneda, 1981
13. See Stevens, 1983, chapter 8, on the Father archetype.

Chapter Six: Dreaming Dasein

1. Boss, 1958, 1977a, 1977b
2. Boss, 1977b, p. 18-26
3. Some seminal works that aid understanding of the Continental tradition are Smith and McIntyre's (1982) Fregean interpretation of Husserl, Dreyfus' (1979) existential approach to artificial intelligence, Ricouer's (1970) discussion of Freud and hermeneutics, and Ihde's (1977) demonstration of experimental phenomenology.
4. See the translator's preface to Heidegger's (1954(1972)) *What is called thinking?*
5. See Fodor and Pylyshn (1981)
6. Ricoeur, 1970
7. See Vallicella (1981)
8. Boss, 1977b
9. Gendlin, 1977 and Alderman, 1977
10. Gendlin, 1977. p. 59, bracket added
11. Ibid, p. 62
12. Ibid, p. 64
13. Ibid, p. 66
14. Ibid, p. 71
15. Boss, 1977b, p. 10
16. Ibid, p. 9
17. Boss, 1977a, ps. 64-67
18. Boss, 1977a, p. 182
19. May similarly restricts himself to the dream. (Caligor and May, 1964)
20. Boss, 1977a, ps. 200-202
21. Ibid, p. 207
22. Fodor, 1980
23. The attempt to get outside oneself has a notorious fate in Godel's undecidability theorem (Nagel and Newman, 1958; Globus, 1979).
24. O'Flaherty, 1984, p. 256
25. Ibid, p. 279
26. Ibid, p. 293
27. Gonda, 1959, p. 168
28. O'Flaherty, 1984, p. 237
29. Ibid, p. 213
30. Ibid, p. 294

Epilogue Footnotes

1. Castaneda, 1984
2. Ricoeur, 1970
3. O'Flaherty, 1984, p. 299
4. David Sibley pointed out this positive note to me.

Bibliography

Alderman, H. (1977): The dreamer and the world. In: On dreaming. An encounter with Medard Boss. C.E. Scott, ed., Chico, CA: Scholars Press.

Anderson, J.R. (1983): The architecture of cognition. Cambridge: Harvard University Press.

Arendt, H. (1978): Heidegger at eighty. In: Heidegger and modern philosophy. M. Murray, ed., New Haven: Yale University Press.

Aserinsky, E. and Kleitman, N. (1953): Regularly appearing periods of eye motility and concomitant phenomena. Science 118:273-274.

Aserinsky, E. and Kleitman, N. (1955): Two types of ocular motility occurring during sleep. J. applied physiology 8:1-10.

Bohm, D. (1980): Wholeness and the implicate order. Boston: Routledge and Kegan Paul.

Bolter, J.D. (1984): Turing's man. Chapel Hill: U. of No. Carolina Press.

Boss, M. (1958): The analysis of dreams. A.J. Pomerans, trans., New York: Philosophical Library.

Boss, M. (1977a): "I dreamt last night..." S. Conway, trans., New York: Gardner Press.

Boss, M. (1977b): Dreaming and the dreamed. In: On dreaming. An encounter with Medard Boss. C. E. Scott, Ed. Chico, CA: Scholars Press.

Caligor, L. and May, R. (1968): Dreams and symbols: Man's unconscious language. New York: Basic Books.

Castaneda, C. (1969): The teachings of don Juan: A Yaqui way of knowledge. Berkeley: University of California Press.

Castaneda, C. (1971): A separate reality. New York: Simon and Shuster.

Castaneda, C. (1973): Journey to Ixtlan. New York: Simon and Shuster.

Castaneda, C. (1974): Tales of power. New York: Simon and Shuster.

Castaneda, C. (1978): The second ring of power. New York: Simon and Shuster.

Castaneda, C. (1981): The eagle's gift. New York: Simon and Shuster.

Castaneda, C. (1984): The fire from within. New York: Simon and Shuster.

Cavanagh, J.P. (1975): Two classes of holographic processes realizable in the neural realm. In: Formal aspects of cognitive processes. T. Storer and D. Winter, eds., New York: Springer-Verlag.

Cavanagh, J.P. (1984): Image transforms in the visual system. In: Figural synthesis. Peter C. Dodwell and Terry Gaelli, eds., Hillsdale, N.J.: Lawrence Erlbaum Associates.

Cavanagh, J.P. (1985): Local log polar frequency analysis in the striate cortex as a basis for size and orientation invariance. In: Models of the visual cortex. D. Rose and V.G. Dobson, eds., New York: John Wiley & Sons Ltd.

Chappell, V.C. (1977): Remembering dreams. In: Philosophical essays on dreaming. C. Dunlop, ed. Ithaca: Cornell University Press.

Chomsky, N. (1980): Rules and representations. New York: Columbia University Press.

Clark, A. (1984): Seeing and summing: Implications of computational theories. Cognition and brain theory 7:1-23.

Comay, R. (1986): After metaphysics: On the way to Heidegger. Man and world 19:225-240.

Crick, F. and Mitchison, G. (1983): The function of dream sleep. Nature 304:111-114.

Dement, W.C. and Kleitman, N. (1957): Cyclic variations in EEG during sleep and their relation to eye movements, bodily motility and dreaming. Electroencephalography and clinical neurophysiology 9:673-690.

Dennett, D.C. (1978): Brainstorms: Philosophical essays on mind and psychology. Vermont: Bradford Books Publishers, Inc.

Descartes, R. (1912): Philosophical works of Descartes. Vol. I. E.S. Haldane and G.R.T. Ross, trans., Cambridge: Cambridge University Press.

Dreyfus, H. (1979): What computers can't do. (2nd ed.) New York: Harper and Row.

Dreyfus, H. and Dreyfus, S. (1986): Mind over machine. New York: The Free Press.

Dunlop, C. (1977): Introduction. In: Philosophical essays on dreaming. C. Dunlop, ed., Ithaca: Cornell University Press.

Edelman, G. (1978): Group selection and phasic reentrant signaling: A theory of higher brain functioning. In: The mindful brain. G. Edelman and V.B. Mountcastle, Cambridge: MIT Press.

Edelson, M. (1973): Language and dreams. The psychoanalytic study the child 27:203-282.

Erdelyi, M. (1985): Psychoanalysis. Freud's cognitive psychology. New York: W.H. Freeman.

Evans, L. (1984): Landscapes of the night. P. Evans, ed., New York: Viking Press.

Farber, M. (1943): The foundation of phenomenology, 3rd ed. Albany: State University of New York Press. (p. 203)

Fodor, J.A. (1980): Methodological solipsism considered as a research strategy in cognitive psychology. Behavioral and brain sciences 3:63-73.

Fodor, J.A. and Pylyshn, Z.W. (1981): How direct is visual perception? Some reflections on Gibson's "ecological approach". Cognition 9:139-196.

Foulkes, D. (1978): A grammar of dreams. New York: Basic Books.

Foulkes, D. (1982): A cognitive-psychological model of REM dream production. Sleep 5:169-187.

Foulkes, D. (1985): Dreaming: A cognitive-psychological analysis. Hillsdale, N.J.: Lawrence Erlbaum Associates.

Freud, S. (1900(1953)): The Interpretation of dreams. Standard Edition, vols. 4 and 5. J. Strachey, trans., London: The Hogarth Press.

Freud, S. (1917(1977)): Introductory lectures on psychoanalysis. New York: W.W. Norton (Liveright).

Freud, S. (1923(1953)): Remarks on the theory and practice of dream interpretation. Standard Edition 19:109-121. J. Strachey, trans. London: The Hogarth Press.

Fromm, E. (1957): The forgotten language: An introduction to the understanding of dreams, fairy tales and myths. New York: Grove Press.

Garfield, P. (1974): Creative dreaming. New York: Ballantine Books.

Gendlin, E.T. (1977): Phenomenological concept vs. phenomenological method. In: On dreaming. An encounter with Medard Boss. C.E. Scott, ed. Chico, CA: Scholars Press.

Gibson, J.J. (1966): The senses considered as perceptual systems. Boston: Houghton Mifflin.

Gibson, J.J. (1979): The ecological approach to visual perception. Boston: Houghton Mifflin.

Glass, A. (1984): Materials for optical information processing. Science 226:657-662.

Globus, G. (1970a): Quantification of the sleep cycle as a rhythm. Psychophysiology 7:15-19.

Globus, G., Phoebus, E. and Moore, C. (1970b): REM "sleep" manifestations during waking. Psychophysiology 7:308.

Globus, G. (1979): Is there a ghost in the machine after all? International journal of general systems 5:198.

Globus, G. (1981): Science and sorcery. (German) In: The scientist and the irrational, Vol. I, H. Duerr, ed., Dordrecht-Holland: D. Reidel.

Globus, M. and Globus, G. (1983): The man of knowledge. In: Beyond health and normality, R. Walsh and D. Shapiro, Jr., eds., New York: Van Nostrand Reinhold Co.

Globus, G. (1985): Holonomic theories of brain functioning. NIMHANS Journal (Bangalore) 3:1-6.

Globus, G. (1986): The machine basis for the Dasein: On the prospects for an existential functionalism. Man and world, 19:55-72.

Globus, G. (1987): Three holonomic approaches to the brain. In: Quantum Implications, B. Hiley and D. Peat, eds., London: Routledge and Kegan Paul.

Globus, G. (1986a): Temporality in dreams: A Heideggerian critique of Dennett's dream theory. J. of the British society for phenomenology, 19:186-192.

Gonda, J. (1959): Four Studies in the language of the *Veda*. The Hague.

Greenberg, R. (1970): Dreaming and memory. Int. psychiatric clinics 7:258-267.

Grene, M. (1967): Heidegger. In: The encyclopedia of philosophy, Vol. 3, P. Edwards, ed., New York: MacMillan and The Free Press.

Grossberg, S. (1980): How does a brain build a cognitive code? Psychological review 87:1-51

Gupta, K.D. (1971): The shadow world. A study of ancient and modern dream theories. Delhi: Atma Ram & Sons.

Gurwitsch, A. (1964): Field of consciousness. Pittsburgh: Duquesne University Press.

Hartmann, H. (1939(1958)): Ego psychology and the problem of adaptation. D. Rapaport, trans., New York: International Universities Press.

Haugeland, J. (1982): Weak supervenience. American philosophical quarterly 19:93-103.

Haugeland, J. (1985): Artifical intelligence. The very idea. Cambridge, Mass: MIT Press.

Heidegger, M. (1926(1962)): Being and time. J. Macquarrie and E. Robinson, trans., New York: Harper and Row.

Heidegger, M. (1927(1982)): The basic problems of phenomenlogy. A. Hofstadter, trans., Bloomington: Indiana University Press.

Heidegger, M. (1954(1972)): What is called thinking? J.G. Gray, trans., New York: Harper and Row.

Henderson, J. (1963): The wisdom of the serpent. New York: G. Braziller.

Hobson, J.A. and McCarley, R.W. (1977): The brain as a dream state generator: An activation-synthesis hypothesis of the dream process. American journal of psychiatry 134:1335-1348.

Hooker, M. (ed) (1982): Leibniz: Critical and interpretive essays. Minneapolis: University of Minnesota Press.

Hopfield, J.J. and Tank, D.W. (1986): Computing with neural circuits: A model. Science 233:625-633.

Husserl, E. (1913(1931)): Ideas: General introduction to pure phenomenology, W.R. Gibson, trans., New York: MacMillan.

Husserl, E. (1931(1960)): Cartesian meditations. D. Cairns, trans., The Hague: Martins Nijhoff.

Ihde, D. (1977): Experimental phenomenology. New York: C.P. Putman & Sons.

Jerne, N.K. (1967): Antibodies and learning: Selection versus instruction. In: The neurosciences: A study program, G.C. Quarton, T. Melnechuk, and F. O. Schmitt, eds., New York: Rockefeller Press.

Jerne, N.K. (1973): The immune system. Scientific American 229:52-60.

Jerne, N.K. (1974): Towards a network theory of the immune system. Annales immunology (Inst. Pasteur) 125C:373-389.

Jerne, N.K. (1984): Idiotypic networks and other preconceived ideas. Immunological review 79:5-24.

Jerne, N.K. (1985): The generative grammar of the immune system. Science 229:1057-1059.

Jerne, N.K., Roland, J. and Cazenaue, P.A. (1982): Recurrent idiotopes and internal images. The EMBO Journal 1:243-247.

Jung, C.G. (1953): Psychological reflections. (Bollinger Series XXXI) New York: Pantheon Books.

Jung, C.G. (1960): The structure and dynamics of the psyche. Vol. 8, Collected Works, R. Hull, trans., New York: Pantheon Books.

Jung, C.G. (ed) (1964): Man and his symbols. Garden City, NY: Doubleday and Co.

Jung, C.G. (1974): Dreams. R.F.G. Hull, trans., Bollinger Series. Princeton, NJ: Princeton University Press.

Kerr, N., Foulkes, D., and Schmidt, M. (1982): The structure of laboratory dream reports in blind and sighted subjects. Journal of nervous and mental disease 170:286-294.

Kleitman, N. (1982): Basic rest-activity cycle—22 years later. Sleep 5:311-317.

Kosslyn, S.M. (1980): Image and mind. Cambridge, Mass.: Harvard Univ. Press.

Kripke, D. and Sonnenschein, D. (1978): A biologic rhythm in waking fantasy. In: The stream of consciousness. K.S. Pope and J.L. Singer eds., New York: Plenum Press.

Kundera, M. (1984): The unbearable lightness of being. M. Heim, trans., New York: Harper and Row.

LaBerge, S. (1985): Lucid dreaming. Los Angeles: J.P. Tarcher.

Lashley, K.S. (1929): Brain mechanisms and intelligence. Chicago: University of Chicago Press.

Leder, J. (1982): The genetics of antibody diversity. Scientific American 246:102-115.

Leger, J.R. and Lee, S.H. (1982): Hybrid optical processor for pattern recognition and classification using a generalized set of pattern functions. Applied Optics 27:274-287.

Leibniz, G.W. (1951): Leibniz: Selections. P.P. Wiener, trans., New York: Scribners.

McCarley, R.W. and Hobson, J.A. (1977): The neurobiological origins of psychoanalytic dream theory. American journal of psychiatry 134:1211-1221.

Mahoney, P. and Singh, R. (1975): *The interpretation of dreams.* Semiology and Chomskian linguistics. Psychoanalytic study of the child 30:221-241.

Malcolm, N. (1959): Dreaming. New York: Humanities Press.

Mandler, G. (1985): Cognitive psychology. Hillsdale, N.J.: Lawrence Erlbaum Associates.

Marrack, P. and Kappler, J. (1986): The T cell and its receptor. Scientific American 254:36-45.

Merleau-Ponty, M. (1962): The phenomenology of perception. C. Smith, trans., London: Routledge and Kegan Paul.

Moline, J. (1981): Plato's theory of understanding. Madison: University of Wisconsin Press.

Nagel, E. and Newman, J. (1958): Godel's proof. New York: New York University Press.

Natsoulas, T. (1984): Freud and Consciousness I. Intrinsic consciousness. Psychoanalysis and contemporary thought 7:195-232.

Natsoulas, T. (1985): Freud and consciousness II. Derived consciousness. Psychoanalysis and contemporary thought 8:183-220.

Neisser, U. (1967): Cognitive psychology. New York: Meredith Publishing Co.

Neisser, U. (1976): Cognition and reality. San Francisco: W.H. Freeman.

Newell, A. (1973): Production systems: Models of control structures. In: Visual information processing. W. Chase, ed., New York: Academic Press.

O'Flaherty, W.D. (1984): Dreams, illusion and other realities. Chicago: University of Chicago Press.

Pepper, D. (1986) Applications of optical phase conjugation. Scientific American 254:74-83.

Perls, F. (1969): Gestalt therapy verbatim. Lafayette, CA: Real People Press.

Peterfreund, E. (1971): Information, systems and psychoanalysis. New York: International Universities Press.

Pietsch, P. (1981): Shufflebrain. Boston: Houghton Mifflin.

Pribram, K. (1971): Languages of the brain. Englewood Cliffs: Prentice Hall.

Pribram, K., Nuwer, M. and Baron, R.J. (1974): The holographic hypothesis of memory structure in brain function and perception. In: Contemporary developments in mathematical psychology, Vol. II. R.C. Atkinson, D.H. Krantz, R.C. Luce, and P. Suppes, eds., San Francisco: W.H. Freeman.

Pylyshn, Z.W. (1981): The imagery debate: Analogue media versus tacit knowledge. Psychological review, 88:16-45.

Pylyshn, Z.W. (1984): Computation and cognition. Cambridge: MIT Press.

Rechtschaffen, A. (1978): The single-mindedness and isolation of dreams. Sleep 1:97-109.

Ricoeur, P. (1970): Freud and philosophy: An essay on interpretation. D. Savage, trans., New Haven: Yale University Press.

Ricoeur, P. (1978): The task of hermeneutics. In: Heidegger and modern philosophy. M. Murray, ed., New Haven: Yale University Press.

Rock, I. (1983): The knowledge of perception. Cambridge: MIT Press.

Sartre, J.P. (1940(1961)): The psychology of imagination. Secaucus: The Citadel Press.

Scott, C.E. (1977): Medard Boss. In: On dreaming. An encounter with Medard Boss. C.E. Scott, ed., Chico, CA: Scholars Press.

Searle, J.R. (1980): Minds, brains, and programs. Behavioral and brain sciences 3:417-457.

Searle, J.R. (1983): Intentionality: An essay in the philosophy of mind. Cambridge: Cambridge University Press.

Searle, J.R. (1984): Minds, brain and science. Cambridge: Harvard University Press.

Sellars, W. (1963): Science, perception and reality. New York: The Humanities Press.

Siegler, F.A. (1977): What dreams are made on. In: Philosophical essays on dreaming. C. Dunlop, ed., Ithaca: Cornell University Press.

Smith, Q. (1977): A phenomenological examination of Husserl's theory of hyletic data. Philosophy today 21:356-357.

Smith, D. W. (1982): The realism in perception. Nous 16:42-55.

Smith, D.W. and McIntyre, R. (1982): Husserl and intentionality. Boston: D. Reidel Publishing Co.

Stark, H. (ed) (1982): Applications of optical Fourier transforms. New York: Academic Press.

Stroke, G.W. (1969): An introduction to coherent optics and holography, 2nd ed., New York: Academic Press.

Stevens, A. (1983): Archetypes. A natural history of the self. New York: Quill.

Tonegawa, S. (1985): The molecules of the immune system. Scientific American 253:122-131.

Vallicella, W. (1981): The problem of being in the early Heidegger. The Thomist, 45:388-406.

van Dam, A. (1984): Computer software for graphics. Scientific American 251:146-159.

Vander Lugt, A. (1964): IEEE transactions in information theory. IT-10:139-145.

Weimer, W. (1973): Psycholinguistics and Plato's paradoxes of the *Meno*, American psychologist 28:15-33.

Westerlundh, B. and Smith, G. (1983): Percept genesis and the psychodynamics of perception. Psychoanalysis and contemporary thought 6:597-640.

Wijsenbeek-Wijler, H. (1978): Aristotle's concept of soul, sleep and dreams. Amsterdam: Adolph M. Hakkert.

Wilber, K. (1982): Physics, mysticism and the new holographic paradigm. In: The holographic paradigm and other paradoxes, K. Wilber, ed., Boulder: Shambhala.

Wittgenstein, L. (1958): Philosophical investigations. G.E.M Anscombe, trans., New York: The MacMillan Co.

Yevick, M. (1975): Holographic or Fourier logic. Pattern recognition 7:197-213.

Subject Index

Name Index